FEDERATION SQUARE

Hardie Grant Books

This edition published in 2005
First published in 2003
by Hardie Grant Books
85 High Street
Prahran, Victoria 3181, Australia
www.hardiegrant.com.au

National Library of Australia Cataloguing-in-Publication Data:

Day, Norman.
Federation Square.

Updated ed.
ISBN 1 74066 313 6.

1. Federation Square (Melbourne, Vic.). 2. Public architecture – Victoria – Melbourne. 3. Public works – Victoria – Melbourne. I. Brown-May, Andrew, 1961– . II. Title.

711.558

Edited by Clare Coney
Photography by Trevor Mein unless otherwise attributed
Cover and text design by Trampoline
Printed and bound in China by SNP Leefung

10 9 8 7 6 5 4 3 2 1

To all those who helped realise Federation Square

CONTRIBUTORS

Dr Andrew Brown-May teaches in the History Department at the University of Melbourne and is director of the Encyclopedia of Melbourne project. His publications include *Melbourne Street Life* (1998) and *Espresso! Melbourne Coffee Stories* (2001).

Professor Dr Norman Day worked with the late Robin Boyd and Professor Frederick Romberg before starting his own practice in 1971. He is an Adjunct Professor of Architecture at the University of RMIT and is architecture critic for *The Age* and ABC (Radio and TV) and author of several books on architecture.

Lab architecture studio and **Federation Square Management** made available many resources to help compile the text for Part II of this book.

Sheep, frocks, vans and bricks. A diploma of fashion design rounded off **Trevor Mein**'s adolescence on a farm in Central Victoria. He photographed cars for custom car magazines through an architectural degree at RMIT. His photos are featured extensively in Australian and overseas publications. www.meinphoto.com

ACKNOWLEDGEMENTS

This book is a tribute to everyone who has been involved in the building of Federation Square.

Several individuals who managed major components from the very start of the project to the end are worthy of special mention: Lab architecture studio's Peter Davidson, Don Bates and Tony Allen; Multiplex's Simon Gray and Tony Hodder; and Federation Square Management's Tjip Faber.

We would also like to acknowledge those who have specifically helped make this tribute happen:

At Federation Square Management we would like to thank Peter Seamer and Stan Liacos.

At Lab architecture studio we would like to thank all those in the office who have helped download images, supply plans and resource material.

We would also like to thank Andrew Brown-May and Norman Day for their words; Clare Coney for bringing together the text in Part II, as well as her invaluable editing skills; Sean Hogan at Trampoline for his design; Trevor Mein, Peter Clarke, John Gollings, Andrew Hobbs, John Donegan and Stuart Milligan for their images.

Federation Square Management would like to sincerely thank the thousands of people that helped make Federation Square a reality. In particular we wish to acknowledge the State Government of Victoria that had the courage to commence and complete a project of the scale and nature of Federation Square with the support of the City of Melbourne, the Commonwealth Government and the private sector through the Square's various commercial tenancies and sponsorship partners.

I   HISTORY AND DEVELOPMENT OF THE SITE

Andrew Brown-May

INTRODUCTION

After flowing on in silence and solitude for some thousand years, the Yarra has suddenly seen a populous city, 'rise like an exhalation' on its banks. Fourteen years have not yet elapsed since Melbourne was founded; yet it has already passed through three stages of progress. First, there was the primeval period of wattle-and-dab; then came the era of weather-boarding and broad paling. From this we are now rapidly emerging to the solid substantiality of brick and mortar. Whatever, therefore, is done NOW must give it impress to the FUTURE. This then is the golden opportunity for improvement, which, if neglected, will never return. Every year that the work is postponed the sacrifice demanded will augment, while its fruits will become less and less. Let us not then in our practice realize the fable of the Sibylline leaves. We know not who may be the first Governor of Victoria: but whoever he may be, we hope that if he cannot achieve the boast of Augustus, – "Urbem Marmoream se relinquere quam lateritiam accepisset," his vice-royalty may yet be distinguished by such a complete re-modelling of the city, that, when he leaves us, we may inscribe to his memory, in the future Great Square of the City, the proud epitaph of Wren under the cupola of St. Paul's, "IF YOU ASK FOR HIS MONUMENT – LOOK AROUND YOU."

[Anonymous, Melbourne as it is, and as it ought to be; with remarks on street architecture generally, Reprinted from the first number of The Australasian, Revised, Melbourne: J. Pullar; Geelong: J. Harrison, 1850.]

Surveyor Robert Hoddle's plan setting out Melbourne's streets in a grid has for over a century and a half guided and fashioned Melbourne's incremental growth and development. As an abstract symbol the grid has also stood for the city itself: open, ordered, civilised, approachable. But as the anonymous critic of 1850 pointed out in criticising the lack of an open square – 'one of the first requirements of a town' – the people of Melbourne have long bewailed the straitjacket of the grid and the lack of a grand open space.

At various times over Melbourne's history, architects and visionaries have teased the citizens with plans for such a civic place. Federation Square could therefore be regarded as the realisation of a long dream, the practical culmination of 150 years of vision and revision.

This new square promises to be not just any place. It is a necessary space, both as a place where Melburnians can gather in large numbers, and as an architectural focus. It is sited in the logical place, at Melbourne's southern gateway, which is redolent with history and inherited meaning. This stretch of land has, from the moment it was set aside for public purposes by Melbourne's early surveyors, been at the intersection of the city's comings and goings. It is at the confluence of road, rail and river – bounded by Swanston Street and Princes Bridge to the west, Flinders Street to the north and the river to the south. It has rubbed shoulders with market, morgue, church and hotel, and it has borne constant witness to the life and death of the city and the daily affairs of its visitors and inhabitants.

The anonymous critic quoted to the left, writing on the cusp of Victoria's official separation from New South Wales in 1851, recorded with uncanny prescience the difficulties that would attend any attempt to perform major alterations to Hoddle's original plan over the ensuing 150 years. The final realisation of the Federation Square project at the city's southern threshold promises to be a long-awaited monument to Melbourne's public life.

Aerial site photograph
State Government, Design Competition package

EARLY DAYS: 1835–54

Aboriginal Peoples

At the time of first European settlement in the Melbourne region, the Kulin confederacy of Aboriginal peoples comprised five language groups whose domain was the broad Port Phillip region. Three groups had territory bordering Port Phillip Bay – the Wathaurung, the Bunurong and the Woiworung. The Woiworung group, itself comprising a number of clans including the Wurundjeri, laid claim to the area drained by the Yarra River and its tributaries. In the first years after European settlement in Melbourne, Aboriginal clans would sometimes camp at their traditional locations on both sides of the Yarra, at spots near the future Melbourne Cricket Ground and Government House. As late as January 1870 one report noted that Aborigines were camped on the reserve later to be occupied by the railway yards, just south of Russell Street.

Land Sales

Land north of Flinders Street and west of Swanston Street was sold as subdivisions at the first government land sale, on 1 June 1837. Land to the east of Swanston Street was sold at the third sale, on 13 September 1838. In 1838 the land where Federation Square now stands, to the south of Flinders Street, from its eastern corner with Swanston Street across to the Police Magistrate's Paddock level with Gisborne Street, was reserved for public purposes. This land, a low-lying swampy paddock sloping down to the Yarra River with a lagoon that filled whenever the river overflowed, was soon enclosed by post-and-rail fences.

Pound and Punt

In March 1839 Captain William Lonsdale, Superintendent and first Police Magistrate of the Port Phillip District, appointed George Scarborough to be Keeper of the Pound on part of the Reserve 'situate midway between the western boundary of the Police Magistrate's Paddock and the punt of the Yarra River, and at the distance of about fifty feet from the edge of the right bank of the River Yarra'. According to historian W.H. Newnham, a well-known personality at the pound was a magpie nicknamed 'Professor' who was partial to hard liquor, was known to put in a bid at auctions, and drowned in the Yarra 'under the influence'.

An early settler, Arundel Wrighte, had erected a weatherboard house in the Police Magistrate's Paddock – also known as the Government Paddock – at the eastern end of the town, and though instructed by William Lonsdale under the Crown Lands Occupation Act to remove the house in 1837, remained in situ until 1839. Early in 1838 Thomas Watt had established a punt which he christened *The Melbourne*, running across the river some way above the Falls (the Falls was a small rocky reef or ledge across the Yarra, a little to the west of present-day Queen Street, above which the river was fresh water; the Falls were removed in 1883). Later operated by John Welsh, 'Garryowen' gives its location in *Chronicles of Early Melbourne* as being halfway between Swanston and Russell streets. An 1870s painting by W.F.E. Liardet, recalling the scene of the first punt, also shows a house on the north bank of the Yarra which is possibly Alexander Thomson's, as shown on Robert Russell's 1837 plan of Melbourne.

Flinders Street looking east from Swanston Street, 1913–14
La Trobe Picture Collection, State Library of Victoria

Soon the partially completed complex was being used as the City Coroner and Registrar's office, but not as a morgue, and in June 1856 it was recorded that access to the Office was obstructed both by drays and carts cutting up the footpath as they crossed to the watering place on the Yarra, as well as by noisome piles of rotting animal and vegetable matter.

It is clear that at least until the end of 1854, dead bodies were still being conveyed to public houses, as the question of the morgue's placement had not been settled. An inquest into the death of Alexander McQueen, a boy who had drowned after falling into the race supplying the waterworks at the Spring Street end of Flinders Street (listed in directories until 1870), was held at the Duke of Wellington Hotel on 30 November 1854. The *Argus* again noted the necessity for a proper morgue after 'the friends of the unfortunate lad complained of the body having been deposited in a fowl-house, exposed to the heat of the atmosphere, which induced decomposition so rapidly, as to be painful to them even in the short time elapsing between the death and the inquest'.

Temporary morgues were located at the Australian Wharf and elsewhere, but by 1870 further discussion again took place about finding a more suitable location. In February 1871 the Princes Bridge site was favoured by the *Argus* – rather changing its tune – over other sites which were deemed to be even more noticeable:

The site at the end of King-street – or Queen-street – is really much more conspicuous than that at Prince's-bridge, which, being in a line with the street, and having nothing particular to indicate its character, would be passed by thousands of people without being noticed; whereas at the other place it will be quite detached, and a prominent object for some distance around. The Melbourne Hospital deadhouse is built at the corner of two frequented streets, and I do not think that one person in a thousand knows what it is. I understand that it was intended to have the entrance to the Morgue at the back of the building and out of Flinders-street; so that nothing but a blank wall would have been presented to Swanston-street.

The Princes Bridge Morgue, completed in 1871, was attached to the original 1854 office building. The deadhouse, a building with no windows, was separated from the court building where inquests were held by a yard, while a separate space was specifically designated as a laboratory. The courtroom could be entered from either the yard or the Flinders Street side of the building. If the latter was used, jurors and witnesses would not pass the deadhouse or face the possibility of seeing bodies in the deadhouse. Bodies would most likely have been taken in the side entrance, closest to the deadhouse.

The Morgue was not to stay here long, however. In 1888 it found a more permanent home, just outside the city on Yarra Bank Road (Batman Avenue), where it remained until the 1950s.

The original building was occupied by the Registrar as well as the Coroner, and is listed variously as an office for the registration of births, deaths, marriages, vaccination and electoral purposes. From the time of its initial construction in the 1850s, the law required children to be registered within 60 days of their birth. Parents or occupiers of premises where a birth or death occurred were required to notify the registrar. Deaths were to be registered before the funeral took place, so that the Registrar could give a certificate of registration to the undertaker. By the 1850s parents were also required to have their children vaccinated and to produce them again for inspection eight days afterwards.

In 1859 the Registrar of Births and Deaths and the Electoral Registrar for the District and City of Melbourne was the Hon. J.D. Tierney, M.D., while Melbourne directories list the caretaker of the Registration Office (and from 1871 cum Morgue) from the late 1860s to the early 1880s as Ellen Tierney and Ellen Prendergast. In 1875 Mrs Prendergast was aghast to find the door of the Morgue had been left ajar, and a corpse 'on the slab in the centre of the Morgue... so that any person having occasion to enter the yard would have a full view'.

City Gateway

Even after the central morgue had been established in the city with a courthouse, bodies were still taken to local hotels for inquest. There was also new concern about the propriety of having the Morgue in such a prominent position. By 1878 the dilapidated state of the Morgue induced Coroner Candler to suggest 'that the place should be made far more presentable than it is – more creditable to the City of Melbourne – and more fitted for its purpose'. In a sense this signals a new era of civic consciousness in relation to the public image of the city, and the area south-east of Swanston and Flinders streets came under scrutiny as much as everywhere else.

The railway played a major part in the establishment of the Swanston and Flinders intersection as one of the great hubs of Melbourne. Its siting along the southern side of Flinders Street (discussed further below) meant a reassessment of all the buildings in the area and the Princes Bridge Morgue was abandoned by the coroners in 1883, when the railway department required the old building.

With the building of a new Princes Bridge in 1888 the area had indubitably become the gateway into Melbourne. In 1889 some citizens urged improving the intersection 'to make a truly noble approach to Prince's Bridge'. By 1900 the site was firmly identified as the city's gateway from St Kilda Road, and improvements after 1901 were motivated by the opening of Federal Parliament in Melbourne, the Royal Visit of the Duke of Cornwall and York, later to become King George V, and the visit of the American Fleet in 1908. By 1908, the Melbourne City Council and the Government had invested hundreds of thousands of pounds on a new railway station and on statues, lawns and flowerbeds at the city's southern entrance in an effort, as the *Argus* would have it in 1908, 'to make this spot – the city's front door – a credit to Melbourne'.

The intersection of Swanston and Flinders streets is at the centre of the Melbourne grid's southern edge. It has always been a heavily trafficked area, as it stands at the confluence of road, river and railway and thus was seen as an appropriate place to make a gateway: the opposing landmarks of St Paul's Cathedral and Young and Jackson's Hotel marked it as pre-eminent on both sacred and secular grounds. This reinforced the special prominence of the place in the mental cartography of Melburnians. Where once morgue and fish market had tainted its symbolic primacy, by 1908 these were being replaced by a new and grand central railway station, nearing completion.

PRINCES BRIDGE

Princes Bridge is one of the most important nineteenth-century bridges in Australia and one of Melbourne's best-known landmarks. Considered a major civic and historic structure, Princes Bridge and its predecessors have been popular images of Melbourne, reproduced in artwork and postcards.

The bridge crosses the Yarra River to form a grand southern gateway linking St Kilda Road with Swanston Street. The current bridge is the third on the site, being constructed as the result of an architectural design competition and opened in 1888. At the junction of rail, river and road routes, it continues to be a focus for the social life of the city.

The place where Princes Bridge would later be constructed had been established as the major crossing point of the Yarra River at the very beginning of white settlement. Before the construction of a bridge across the Yarra, punts would carry people and animals from bank to bank here. Since Princes Bridge was built, for well over a century it has been the major access point into the city from the populous south-eastern suburbs, and an important traffic artery, carrying as it does numerous tram lines. It forms part of the major civic axis of Swanston Street. Spanning Melbourne's premier waterway, Princes Bridge is also the main route from the city to the extensive parks – and the Botanic Gardens – on the southern bank of the river, and to the Southbank arts and retail precinct.

Early Bridges

An 1845 timber bridge, only 17 feet (5.18 metres) wide, was leased to a Robert Balbirnie, who profited from the tolls he charged people to cross. On 20 March 1846 Governor La Trobe laid the foundation stone of a new bridge, named after Queen Victoria's young son Edward, Prince of Wales, later King Edward VII.

La Trobe finally opened the bridge on 15 November 1850 as part of the Separation celebrations – in August Queen Victoria had granted Royal Assent to the Australian Colonies Government Act, which provided for the separation of the Port Phillip District, as Victoria was then known, from New South Wales.

Thirty feet (9.14 metres) wide and with a single arch spanning 150 feet (45 metres), the new bridge was only two feet shorter than London Bridge and one of the longest of its kind in the world. However, its life was short. Flooding had been a worry for early Melburnians. Every few decades the Yarra River burst its banks and took furious retribution on those who had built on its floodplain. In 1803, James Flemming, a member of Surveyor Charles Grimes's party, had noted flood marks on trees along the river that were 20 feet (6.10 metres) above the ground. European settlers experienced their first major inundation on Christmas Day 1839 and from then on a fear of floods was a continuing anxiety for nineteenth-century Melbourne. A great flood in December 1863 stretched from the Customs House in Flinders Street (now the Immigration Museum) to present-day Toorak Road.

Major engineering works were undertaken in the 1880s for flood mitigation purposes. One result was doubling the width of the Yarra River, as well as deepening it, and a new bridge was therefore essential. The original width of the river at the site of the bridge at ordinary times had been about 130 feet (39.62 metres) and was increased at the time of construction to about 316 feet (96.32 metres). The second bridge was therefore demolished in 1884 and a temporary bridge conducted Melburnians across the river until the opening of the current bridge to traffic on 4 October 1888.

The foundation stone of the new bridge was laid on 7 September 1886 by Mrs Stewart, wife of the then Mayor of Melbourne. The City of Melbourne contributed one-third of the construction cost of the bridge, the cities of South Melbourne and Prahran and the borough of St Kilda £10,000 each, the shire of Malvern £2,500, the borough of Brighton and the shire of Caulfield £2,000 each, and the shire of Moorabbin £1,000. The design, by architects Grainger and Jenkins, was chosen by competition in 1879, and the bridge was built by the prolific builders David Munro & Co.

Opened on 4 October 1888, the bridge immediately created an impressive gateway into the city from the south. It is notable as one of the major projects of civic embellishment undertaken in the boom years of the 1880s, and is arguably the most grandly conceived and one of the most ornate nineteenth-century bridges in a major city in Australia. Resembling Blackfriars Bridge in London, Princes Bridge is 99 feet (30.18 metres) wide and 400 feet (121.92 metres) long, with three spans of 100 feet (30.48 metres) each and a land span of 24 feet (7.32 metres) at the southern end. The abutments, piers and wing walls are built of bluestone, with concrete foundations resting on solid rock. The bridge absorbed 1,000 tons of wrought iron and 2,000 tons of cast iron in its construction, the cast-iron lamps being added in the 1920s.

View of the opening of the old Princes Bridge, 1850
Henry Nash, lithograph
La Trobe Picture Collection, State Library of Victoria

New Princes Street Bridge, 1907
La Trobe Picture Collection, State Library of Victoria

Ritual Space and Meeting Place

Princes Bridge has always been more than just a traffic artery across the Yarra River. From early days it has been used as the site of major civic ceremonies. A grand procession featured in the celebrations for the laying of the foundation stone of the second bridge, the original Princes Bridge, on 20 March 1846. According to the newspapers, 'a finer procession was never seen in any part of the world', and the bridge's construction heralded 'a new era in the annals of Port Phillip history'. The 1867 visit of the Duke of Edinburgh saw the bridge decorated with flags and a celebratory arch, popular features of civic festivity at the time, which featured again on Princes Bridge during the 1901 Commonwealth Celebrations and the 1984 Victorian sesquicentenary.

When Melburnians were not crossing the bridge as part of their daily business, they might stroll across it at a more leisurely pace, taking in the views of the city from its parapets. Along with the steps of Flinders Street Station and the Town Hall corner, the bridge has been a favourite meeting place for generations of Melburnians. Diving, swimming and life-saving displays were popular at the bridge from the 1920s, and from the 1950s Moomba events would use the bridge as stage and stand. The landing below was the starting point for popular inter-war river cruises and excursion services to the Hawthorn Tea Gardens, Dight's Falls, Williamstown and the Maribyrnong.

However, the bridge was not always a source of pleasure to respectable Melburnians. Until 1883 the old city Morgue and Coroner's Office stood on the riverbank to the bridge's east, where many a drowned soul was taken after being dragged out of the Yarra's murky depths. In addition, the poor lighting of the bridge and its surrounds was a common source of complaint about prostitutes and drunken sailors, and although gas lamps were first erected in the 1850s, the bridge's gloomy recesses could harbour all manner of imagined vices and nuisances. The drunken sailors did not have far to go: Princes Bridge Hotel, now more popularly known as Young and Jackson's, was opened at the corner of Swanston and Flinders streets in 1861.

Considered a major civic and historic structure in Melbourne, Princes Bridge has featured in paintings, photographs and postcard views of Melbourne landmarks. Ludwig Becker's 'Old Prince's Bridge and St Paul's by Moonlight' (1857) captured the newly installed gas lamps dominating the night-time scene, and was used as a measure of Melbourne's progress from a frontier town to a provincial metropolis. Four years later Henry Burn painted a daytime view of Swanston Street from Princes Bridge, peopling the bridge's approaches with fashionable townsfolk. Nineteenth-century illustrated journals regularly featured the bridge as a backdrop to the events of the day: Easter Monday river carnivals, rowing regattas, citizens returning home over the bridge at day's end, the decorations and arches that accompanied festival celebrations, or the Yarra River in flood.

Artists' impressions of the new 1880s bridge, as well as depictions of work in progress, were presented to the public along with detailed descriptions of the bridge's specifications and architectural features. Early twentieth-century postcard views featured the City Council Arch for the 1901 visit of the Duke and Duchess of Cornwall and York, the adjacent Snowden and Alexandra Gardens, and picturesque views across the river featuring the bridge and the Melbourne skyline. Today Princes Bridge continues to set the scene at Melbourne's southern entrance, being a visual link to the Shrine of Remembrance from Swanston Street and St Kilda Road, and adjacent to the late-twentieth-century developments at Southbank and Federation Square.

Princes Bridge, 1968
John Collins, photograph
La Trobe Picture Collection, State Library of Victoria

THE YARRA RIVER

Whether celebrated as the 'mother stream of the village of Melbourne' or denigrated as a 'two-faced river' – the *Herald* describing it as both in the mid-twentieth century – Melbourne's location was undoubtedly determined by the existence and the characteristics of a modest river we now know as the Yarra. The availability of fresh water above rocky falls at a site on the river ten kilometres from its mouth persuaded John Batman in 1835 that 'this will be the place for a village'. Any commercial settlement in the early nineteenth century needed fresh water to drink and salt water upon which to float its trading ships, so from the beginning European eyes looked upon the Yarra to assess its utility. Robert Hoddle had soon pegged out his city grid to align with the course of this useful river.

While John Batman's map called it 'Batman's River', its eventual naming is attributed to J.H. Wedge, surveyor for Batman's Port Phillip Association. Wedge's notebook recorded the name 'Yarrow Yarrow', a rendering of 'Yarra Yarra', though he later conceded that he had confused the Aboriginal term for rapids or waterfalls with the name of the river itself. The Aboriginal peoples of the Melbourne region had their own name for the river, recorded as Birrarung.

As Melbourne spread rapidly ferries and then bridges spanned the river, allowing the free movement of people and commerce. Upstream of the growing city water-using industries – fellmongers, wool washers, tanneries and other noxious trades – clustered along the banks of the Yarra. The river was not only used by them as a source of water for processing but also as a convenient place to dispose of their waste, and so an accumulating cargo of rotting animal parts, household rubbish and other pollutants flowed with the stream towards Hobsons Bay.

The river served not only the commercial interests of the town, but was a vital source of potable water. People living in the City of Melbourne were not pleased about the industries upstream, as they drew their drinking water from pumps and risked the ever-present threat of waterborne diseases. In the 1840s pumps had been installed on the north bank between Queen and Russell streets, with others on the north bank in the Police Paddocks between Wellington Parade and the river. In 1854 the inadequacy of the pumps east of Princes Bridge led to long lines of waiting carts. Even in the early years the water quality was often dubious but the water-carts hawked the supply at exorbitant rates. Water supply from the Plenty River via the Yan Yean reservoir system was inaugurated in 1857, bringing piped, clean water to the city, though the water-carts continued to meet local demand into the 1860s.

As well as drinking the water, people bathed in the Yarra River, fished in it and rowed on it for recreation. These conflicting uses of the river degraded it rapidly. Legislation was introduced to combat pollution but it was not effectively enforced. By the 1890s, a Scottish traveller claimed it was 'the filthiest piece of water I ever had the misfortune to be afloat on'. By the end of the century, however, the worst of the abuse was over. Most of the noxious industries had migrated to Footscray and Flemington on the Maribyrnong. Melbourne had belatedly constructed an underground sewerage system in the 1890s, so the city's body wastes now went off to the sewerage farm at Werribee to be treated instead of filtering into the Yarra and its tributaries. Much industrial waste too went into the sewers.

Young and Jackson's Hotel

One of Australia's most famous hotels stands at the north-west corner of Swanston and Flinders streets, on a corner of the block originally purchased by John Batman in 1837 for £100. Part of the allotment was subsequently purchased by Henry Jennings in 1852. By 1853 a three-storey bluestone building had been constructed on the site, occupied on the ground floor by butcher James Graham. On 1 July 1861 John P. Toohey opened the Princes Bridge Hotel. The licence was subsequently transferred to James Hogan (1862) and Joshua Roberts Mooney (1866), and in 1875 taken over by Henry Figsby Young (1845–1925) and Thomas Joshua Jackson (1834–1901), and the hotel became Young and Jackson's. The Dublin-born pair had previously held the licence of the Sparrow's Hotel in St Kilda.

In 1914, Young sold his interests in the hotel to Stephen Morell. Marcel Gilbert purchased the hotel in 1979 for $1,680,000, undertaking extensive renovations, and in 1986 it was purchased by the brewery division of the Bond Corporation. While the building itself has undergone many generations of alterations and extensions, it remains one of Melbourne's principal landmarks at the city's southern gateway. The controversial nude painting of *Chloe* by Parisian Jules Lefebvre was installed in the hotel's saloon bar in 1908, and the building has long been associated with the electric sky-signs above its facade. In the decades following World War II, Dante Triaca operated a restaurant at 'Number One Swanston Street'.

Fish Market

Melbourne's fish market was once located at the south-east corner of Flinders and Swanston streets. A market building was constructed here in 1865, but in 1892 the fish market was moved to new premises at the south-east corner of Spencer and Flinders streets. The old building was demolished in 1900 to make way for the new Flinders Street Station.

St Paul's Cathedral

In 1841 the north-east corner site at the intersection of Swanston and Flinders streets was leased as a hay and corn market, which operated until the 1847 opening of the Eastern Market in Bourke Street. Bishop Charles Perry took the opportunity afforded by the now vacant block to secure a better location for the Church of England in a central and desirable part of town.

The foundation stone of the Charles Webb-designed bluestone St Paul's Church at the corner was laid in 1850, and the building could accommodate 2000 worshippers. However, the site was deemed appropriate for a cathedral, so the original church was demolished in 1885. The cathedral's foundation stone was laid in 1880, and the new cathedral consecrated in 1891. St Paul's Cathedral was designed by English Gothic Revival architect William Butterfield (who never visited Australia).

View looking north along Princes Bridge, 1856
Henry Gritten, La Trobe Picture Collection, State Library of Victoria

View of St Paul's Cathedral (minus spires), ca. 1907
La Trobe Picture Collection, State Library of Victoria

Flinders Street Station, ca. 1920
John Harvey, photograph
La Trobe Picture Collection, State Library of Victoria

Young and Jackson's Hotel, 1977
John Collins, photograph
La Trobe Picture Collection, State Library of Victoria

The growth of railway infrastructure in the mid- to late-nineteenth century paralleled and fed Melbourne's rapid suburban expansion. The Melbourne and Suburban Railway Company operated from the east side of Princes Bridge, first to Richmond from 1857, then to Windsor (1860) and Hawthorn (1861) and from 1859 Princes Bridge Station was the terminus of its Windsor and Brighton lines. The St Kilda and Brighton Railway Company ran a private line between 1857 and 1865.

From 1864 a consolidated company controlling Melbourne's southern and eastern railway traffic became known as the Melbourne and Hobson's Bay United Railway Company. This was taken over by the state-run Victorian Railways Department by 1878. Princes Bridge Station was closed down in 1866 so that its lines could be connected to those running to Flinders Street. To do this culverts were excavated beneath Swanston Street to connect the stations. Lines reopened in 1879 and the station on the east side of Princes Bridge operated as the Victorian Gippsland Railway Station.

Melbourne directories from the 1870s list successive developments at Princes Bridge Station including:
• The parcels office (from 1885)
• Electric Telegraph Office (from 1894)
• Refreshment rooms/confectionery shop (operated by Thomas Gillam from 1897, then Arthur M. Gillam 1908-13)
• A bookshop (Mrs W. Baird in 1887, L. Hume 1891–4, Frank Pyke & Co. 1895–1910 and Gordon & Gotch 1913–8)
• A florist (Moritz Wetheimer 1894)
• Railway Central Booking and Enquiry Office (1903–6)
• Telephone Bureau, Cloak Room and Lost Property Office (from 1908)
• A bootmaker (Harold Sweeney 1927–32, Melbourne Shoe Repairs Pty Ltd 1937–45, City Shoe Repairs Pty Ltd 1946–, Foot Services 1955–62 at 191 Flinders Street)
• A chemist (Whitaker & Cole 1932–7, Dickson's Pharmacy 1938–62, from 1955 at 189 Flinders Street)
• Victorian Railway Sweet Stall (1942–62)
• A fruiterer (from 1955 at 187 Flinders Street).

From 1937 other services were located on the railway concourse, including dry cleaners (Brown's Dry Cleaning 1937–62; Brown Gouge Ltd 1955–), florists (A.S. Wilson 1937–62) and pastrycooks (Scone Cottage 1937–62), and the Victorian Railways Fruit Stall (1946–62). The entrance to the railway station was listed at 267 Flinders Street from 1906, the Electric Telegraph Office at no. 269, while two Post Office receiving pillars (letterboxes) were on the Swanston Street corner.

In 1882 a decision was made to make Flinders Street the city's central railway station, and construction was eventually completed in 1910. It was anticipated that, with the development of the Flinders Street complex, Princes Bridge would thereafter only cater to special race-day and excursion traffic. However, an ever-increasing growth in suburban railway traffic required the continued use of Princes Bridge Station.

View looking west across Jolimont railyards, ca. 1930s.
Photo courtesy of Department of Infrastructure

In 1963 Victorian Premier Henry Bolte announced a £5 million project to roof part of the Princes Bridge railway yards and to build on the roof a plaza and two 15-storey buildings. The project was anticipated as the potential first step in a larger scheme to cover the entire yards with buildings and carparks. The architects were Leslie M. Perrot and Partners; the development company Princes Gate Pty Ltd was jointly owned by Oddenino's Property and Investment Co. Ltd of London and Lend Lease Corporation Ltd of Australia.

By 1966 Melbourne Directories show there was now a development site between the Russell Street Railway entrance and Princes Bridge Station and Kingstrip Carpark. From 1967 the twin towers of the Princes Gate development – regarded by future Melburnians as an eyesore and visual blight – severed the link between Flinders Street east of Swanston Street and the river. The east tower housed the Victorian Employees Federation, the west tower the Gas and Fuel Corporation. Princes Gate Arcade, at the base of the towers, comprised a concourse of 14 shops including a supermarket, clothes shops and a branch of the ANZ Bank. West of Princes Bridge Station and the Kingstrip carpark a public terrace capped off the Swanston Street corner of the site. The twin towers were demolished in 1996–7.

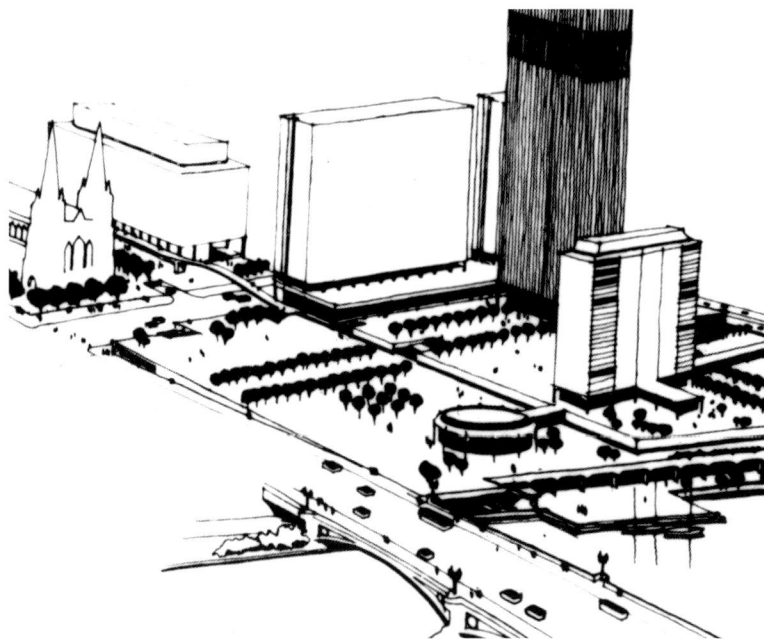

Perspective sketch of Perrott's completed 'scheme' for Princes Bridge, 1963
La Trobe Picture Collection, State Library of Victoria

Gas and Fuel Corporation building, seen
from above Young and Jackson's Hotel, 1967
© Wolfgang Georg Sievers, 1967
Licensed by VISCOPY, Sydney 2003

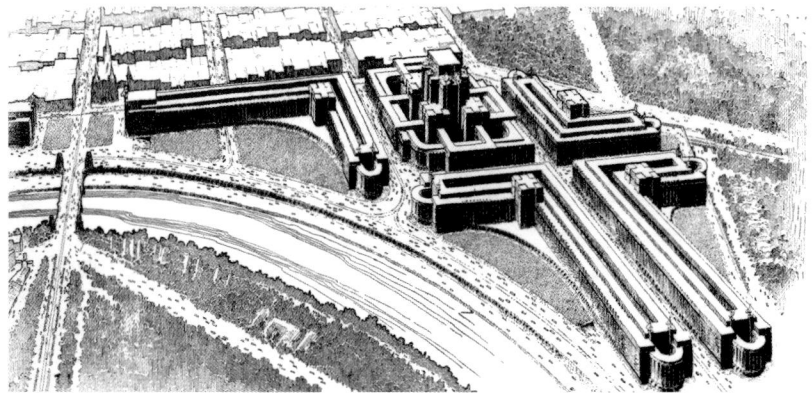

Scheme for a vision of greater Melbourne, 1925
La Trobe Picture Collection, State Library of Victoria

As Melbourne has searched over its history both for a suitable city square site and for a design solution for its important southern gateway, a host of designs – most never realised – have crossed architects' drawing boards. From the speculations of the anonymous critic in 1850, the early-modernist schemes of the 1920s when the town planning profession was in its infancy, through the late-modernist schemes of 1950s, to the post-modernism of the 1990s, the potential of the site as a symbolic gateway and meeting place has been recognised.

The roofing of the rail yards had been mooted at least from the 1920s, and successive proposals offered design solutions including developments that incorporated car parking, terraces, office blocks and civic plazas.

Cathedral Square Proposal

The winner of a design competition sponsored by the Royal Victorian Institute of Architects, architect James Smith's 'Cathedral Square' proposal was announced in 1925. It was a development set back from the street line and comprising a paved civic plaza, fountain, arcaded walk, steps, railway offices, tourist bureau and concourses. The proposal was seen as an opportunity to develop the Princes Bridge Station site so as to be 'worthy of Melbourne's present and future greatness', with 'a clear and uninterrupted vista of the cathedral' and enhancing the beauty of the St Kilda Road approach to Melbourne from the south.

The RVIA had a number of alternative schemes under consideration, which perhaps included R.R. Prentice's Princes Bridge Station redevelopment plan. Proposals for redevelopment of Princes Bridge precinct were further discussed in the Journal of the Royal Victorian Institute of Architects in 1928, the Minister for Railways inviting designs for a new square and decking of the rail yards.

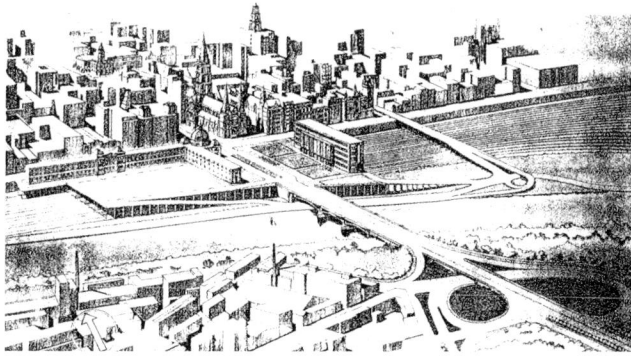

Illustration from 1954 which conforms with 1928 R.V.I.A. committee proposal for Princes Bridge site.

1929   *1954*

Metropolitan Town Planning Commission   *MMBW Melbourne Metropolitan Planning Scheme*

The Metropolitan Town Planning Commission was created in 1922. Chaired by Melbourne City Councillor and architect Frank Stapley, the Commission reported in 1929 on a general outline for Melbourne's urban planning and development. Along with an extensive proposal for covering the Jolimont railway yards, the Report reviewed various proposals that had been submitted for a city square at Princes Bridge. The Victorian Railways Commissioners, with the support of the City Council, had put forward a proposal to build a tourist bureau over the Princes Bridge Railway Station.

The initial scheme was to build over a section of the railway yards east of the bridge, between Flinders Street and Batman Avenue, so that a building could be erected by the Department with a western alignment 33 feet (10.06 metres) east of Princes Bridge. Following public pressure for a larger amount of open space than 33 feet, an expert committee comprising the Metropolitan Engineer of the Railway Department, the Surveyor to the MTPC, the City Engineer and Deputy Town Clerk of the City of Melbourne issued a report on 30 August 1928 recommending that while the provision of a city square was desirable, the proposed location bounded by Swanston and Flinders streets and Batman Avenue was unsuitable, due to the great expenditure and the fact that a square in such a busy traffic centre 'would be entirely unsuitable as a place of assembly on important occasions.'

From 1949 the Melbourne and Metropolitan Board of Works was entrusted with formulating a metropolitan planning strategy for Melbourne, with engineer E.F. Borrie as Chief Planner. The 1954 Melbourne Metropolitan Planning Scheme broached the issue of 'Possible Development in the Vicinity of Princes Bridge', which proposed to upgrade the city's southern gateway by redeveloping the river frontage, partially roofing the rail yards, constructing a bridge from Russell Street to Batman Avenue and building underpasses below Princes Bridge and Batman Avenue.

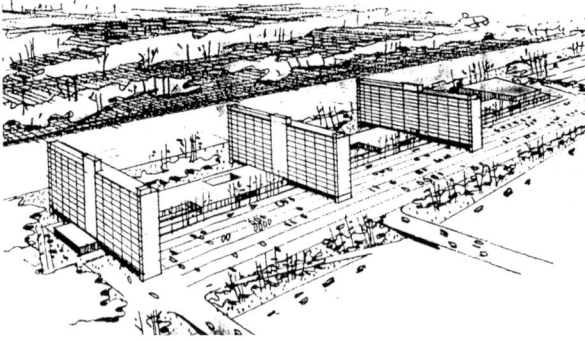

1958	*1961*	*1973*

Kenneth McDonald Plan

Kenneth McDonald and Associates put forward a plan to the Melbourne City Council in 1958 to roof the rail yards between Swanston and Spring streets in a development that included apartment and hotel towers, a theatre and an office tower with shops, open squares, car parks and gardens.

William Lempriere Scheme

The City Development Association, a CBD pressure group of commercial, insurance and other interests, was formed in 1953 to agitate for central city promotion and urban improvement. Executive Director N. Lyncham proposed in 1961 that Princes Bridge was the ideal site for a city square of 'reasonable proportions' that would 'enhance that entrance to the city'. In 1961 wool-broker and ex-Lord Mayor William Lempriere announced his scheme, to be called Matthew Flinders Square. Prepared by architects Montgomery, King and Trengrove and featured on the cover of *Architecture Today* in July 1961, the plan was a response to what Lempriere articulated as the desecration of the city's southern gateway by the rail yards and the 'mid-Victorian monstrosity' of Flinders Street Station. Roofing the rail yards at Princes Bridge and Flinders Street and undergrounding the railway stations would create a large open surface at the city end of Princes Bridge, and enable the construction of a new Town Hall, a six-acre civic square, concert auditoriums, a new railways administration building and other commercial buildings.

Jolimont Pleasure Gardens

The City of Melbourne's 1973 Strategy Plan included a proposal for a 'Jolimont Pleasure Garden' which would involve roofing the Jolimont rail yard to reconnect Melbourne with the Yarra River and the sports and arts precincts beyond.

Lempriere Scheme – Mathew Flinders Square
Montgomery King & Trengrove
La Trobe Picture Collection, State Library of Victoria

1979	1985	1996

Landmark Competition

In August 1979 Victorian Premier Mr Rupert Hamer announced a $100,000 Landmark Competition as part of a larger vision to roof the Jolimont rail yards and a means of capturing international attention to the city. The competition committee, chaired by Ron Walker, chose 48 finalists from around 2,300 entries. The winning designs went on public display in January 1980. No single winner was chosen, the committee generally recommending a composite scheme featuring a large tower in a garden setting. While critics lampooned the competition as an ill-conceived waste of time and resources, each of the 48 finalists received a little over $2,000 prize money.

Judging panel member Professor Patrick McCaughey was quoted as being appalled by the low standard of entries, describing the winners as demonstrations of 'a megalomania that makes the pyramids look like pimples'. Designs for the site included hanging gardens, an underwater gallery, a free-standing escalator, a series of 12 transparent arches, a solar-powered earth beam, a Freedom Bird Park and a Time Tower.

Denton Corker Marshall,
Princes Plaza Proposal

Following an urban design study of the Princes Bridge Station precinct, architects Denton Corker Marshall prepared a scheme for Princes Plaza which entailed demolition of one of the Princes Gate towers and the building of a large street-level plaza stretching across the rail yards. To the east a horizontal block building would enclose a formal garden.

Federation Square

A preliminary Federation Square design brief in 1996 offered worldwide competition entrants the opportunity of producing a design concept for the site that would highlight its fundamental importance as a place of civic celebration and public interaction. The site was conceived in the context of a so-called Federation 'Arc' embracing buildings and sites associated with Australian Federation: the Old Treasury, Treasury Gardens, Parliament House and the Exhibition Buildings.

Photo: John Gollings

II Federation Square

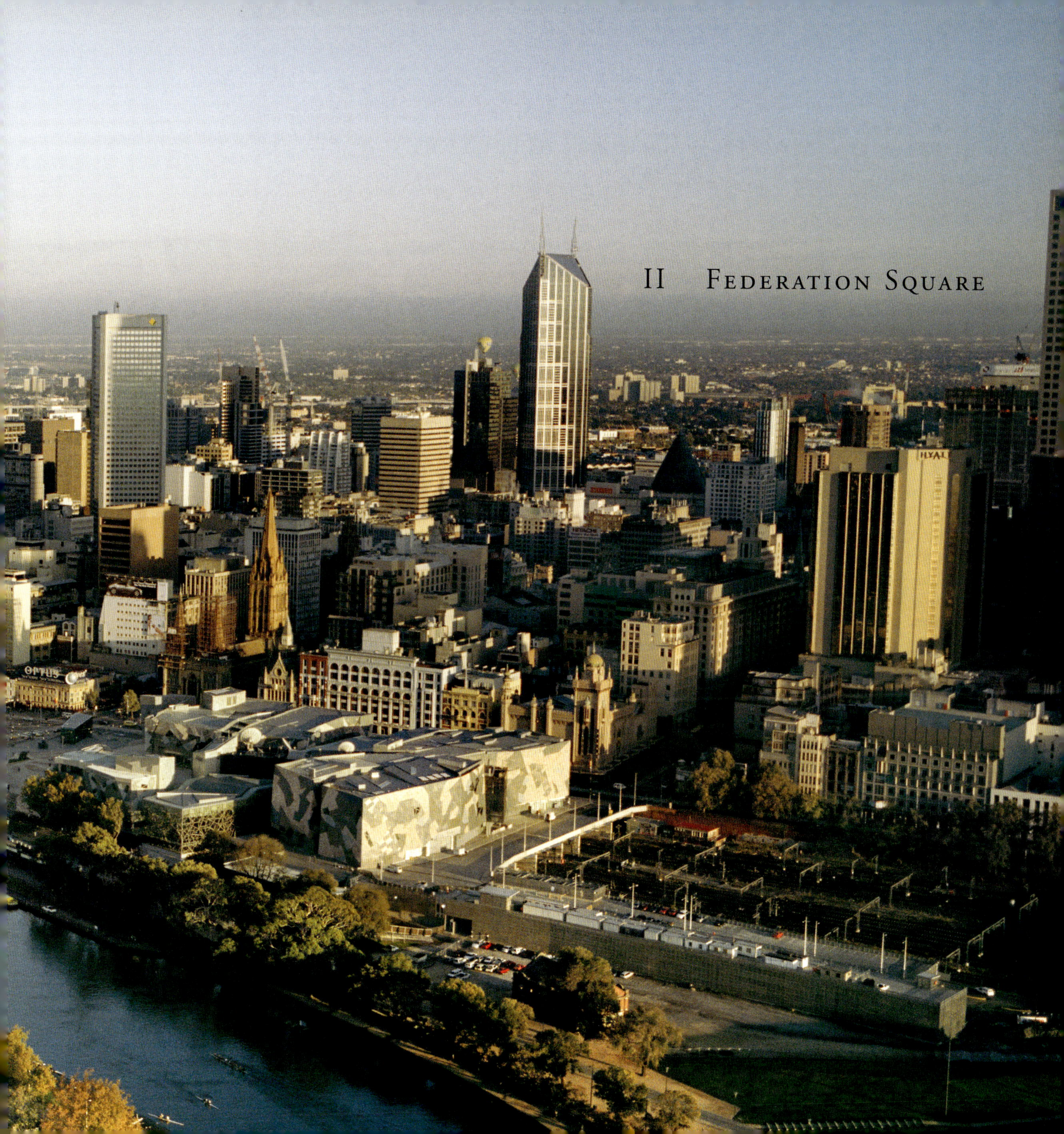

Its authorship is international, even global, while its expression is Australian. The indigenous nature of the architecture comes from a variety of sources – composed using large open spaces, a sparseness, loose form located as if floating in space, aboriginal materials such as the paving and cladding stones, and the capture of sunlight on building surfaces.

It will become an icon in Melbourne, but not like Sydney's Opera House, because Melbourne is composed like a tapestry, with new architectural threads woven into its fabric, where Sydney is made of set pieces arranged around a blue harbour and low hills. One is assimilation the other is exhibition.

There is also more than a suggestion of the Bilbao effect. The extension of the city over old railway yards will ignite other development nearby, the lanes of Melbourne leading to Federation Square will become prime real estate, and the connection to the Yarra River at one of its more alluring points will pay dividends for the citizens who up until now have little chance of connecting with their brown watercourse.

At another level, the Square creates for the first time in the city a sensible and usable large open public space. It may become a civic piazza in time, because it offers open spaces with unrestricted public access, suitable for large public gatherings and celebrations, in a way that Melbourne has lacked. Large gatherings of people will come to call this place home. It is likely to assume the mantle of Melbourne's gathering place, where occasions such as New Year's Eve are celebrated, unionists gather, RSL marches congregate and successful sporting heroes are acclaimed.

There've been four or five competitions held for this site during the 20th century. The last one was held in the late 70s. It was a design competition for a 'landmark'. Melbourne was suffering from what we'd call a 'Sydney Opera House complex'.

Peter Davidson, Lab architecture studio

Lab architecture studio

Lab architecture studio was founded in London in 1994. The principals are Peter Davidson and Donald L. Bates.

Donald Bates, born in Houston, USA, received his Bachelor Degree in architecture from the University of Houston in 1978. In 1980 he undertook a Masters Degree at the prestigious Cranbrook Academy, under the tutelage of renowned architect, Daniel Libeskind. Bates acted as associate architect to Libeskind on both the 'Berlin: City Edge' competition entry, as well as the extension to the Berlin Museum entry (now referred to as the Jewish Museum). He has lectured at the Architectural Association (AA) and founded the independent architectural school, The Laboratory of Primary Studies in Architecture (LoPSiA) in 1990, operating in Paris and at the Le Corbusier Unita d'Habitation, at Briey-en-Foret in France.

Fellow Lab director, Peter Davidson, a native of Newcastle, Australia, graduated from the New South Wales Institute of Technology, Sydney, in 1980. After moving to London in 1981, he was appointed editorial assistant on the journal, *International Architect*. He ran his own practice for ten years while simultaneously teaching at various institutions including the Architectural Association and the respected Bartlett School of Architecture in London. He was visiting critic at many other educational institutions. He has also organised many lecture series at the AA.

Both Don and Peter have taught at numerous universities around the world and both are widely published authors.

Upon winning the 1997 international competition to design Federation Square, Lab established an office in Melbourne while maintaining their London presence. In the five years it took to complete Federation Square, Lab continued to enter selected international competitions and was awarded second place to Zaha Hadid for the BMW Central Building in Leipzig, Germany. They were also short-listed for other prizes, both in Australia and overseas.

Lab continues to extend its efforts to participate in and develop architectural exhibitions and forums. These activities are considered essential by the studio for the continued reinvestment of architectural thought and its professional practice, as well as providing a working basis for architectural research.

Federation Square is Lab architecture studio's most significant project to date and the architects are delighted with how it has been embraced, by Melburnians and visitors alike. It is one of the most significant architectural undertakings in Australia's history and an innovative response to a challenging question.

The layering and patterning of external walls at Federation Square is not unique in Melbourne. ARM's Storey Hall at RMIT developed from similar concerns, but the sheer scale of this development, and especially its three-dimensionality, places it beyond other buildings and much of that is due to the quality of thought underlying the complex ordering of the building surface.

The design of the walls is in fact one large mural, composed as a folded-out graphic then refolded to suit the building forms. Parts are pleated and tucked over the height of the building which creates further shading and light movement. This geometry could also be seen as a concrete metaphor for the planning of the project: there is an equivalence between the two aspects of the architecture – one in two dimensions, the other in 3D.

Lab have layered the walls of the building with internal surfaces, predominantly of glass in frames over a steel frame, with a secondary skin of metal frames, stone panels, metal panels and metal mesh panels. The panels appear tangled and anarchic, but they are all related to each other, so the smallest section of triangulation is a fraction of the largest. It is a repeatable pattern that resounds over the building surface in a way that permeates the building with a regularity, like a piece of music that resonates with a deep thematic rhythm even while it appears to be disordered and hectic.

The result is a surface to the building that is chameleon-like. It changes mood and colour, material and texture at the flick of sunlight or following a brief rain shower.

At night the skin will develop another character via theatrical lighting and the enhancement of spaces made by shadows cast over and around the 'strange' geometries of the Square.

Like most iconic structures, this one will cause images to be invented and metaphors applied. Already there are suggestions of the 'rubbish pile', a Disneyesque 'StrangeWorld', deflated German Expressionism' and more. Doubtless more allegories will follow, and some may make mention of the (reduced) northern shard component of the Square.

Although transparently forced on the project for political rather than architectural reasons, and wrongly so, it is a strangely aggressive little building, like a tourist bus that somehow strayed of the road and sunk into the fabric of the Square.

One characteristic of a fractured geometry is the capacity of a building to grow (or shrink), as if it was never to be completed – a whole of concrete, steel and glass as a living thing – so the city has been provided with an architectural system as much as a fixed building.

At Federation Square, Lab has investigated a proposition for the city as an organism, which is, afterall, the natural way of things.

Late in the 20th century architects followed the leads of poets and musicians, philosophers and politicians, to search for an expression of inclusiveness and diversity. The world had not been explained nor defined by previous simplistic analytical methods nor rational geometric rules. It required a matrix of thought, a changing strategy and a broader grasp of the issues, which is the underlying principle behind Lab's design.

FEDERATION SQUARE

In the 1840s Surveyor Robert Hoddle designed Melbourne's city grid, which has served the city well for over 150 years and also contributed significantly to the widely held belief that Melbourne is a well-designed and well-planned city. However compared with other great cities of the world, there were two features that Melbourne needed to address: to link the central business district to the river, one of its best natural assets, and to create a true public square, a living and breathing focus for the city and its people.

Linking the CBD with the Yarra River had been a continuing dream of Melbourne's planners. The great divide created by the rail yards and the engineering complexities of building over them had thwarted the many and varied proposals for the development of the site.

This divide had also retarded any growth or development of the north bank of the river, unlike the successful Southbank development. Now with these logistical challenges being met through the Federation Square project, Melbourne will become a riverside city and resolve one of its most significant planning deficiencies. The growth and development of Northbank over the next twenty years or so will be interesting to watch.

THE DEVELOPMENT OF FEDERATION SQUARE

The development of Federation Square essentially began in the mid-1990s as part of the Jolimont Rail Yard rationalisation project that reduced the railway lines running parallel to the Yarra River from a total of 53 lines to 12, an initiative made possible by improved railway technologies and the relocation of space-consuming shunting operations to more outlying locations in Melbourne.

Part way through this project, the State Government, in association with the Melbourne City Council, commenced looking at the concept of developing a square over the rail lines. A prerequisite was the removal of the infamous Gas and Fuel towers, two widely disliked buildings that had long exacerbated the physical divide of the city and its river. This initiative opened up the prospect of a larger, more ambitious project which ultimately led to the decision by the State Government and the Council to jointly fund Federation Square and establish an international design competition to determine its appearance and layout.

The Design Competition for Federation Square

Architectural competitions have long been a popular way to build large public projects. In the nineteenth century numerous town halls and public libraries were constructed in the UK and the USA this way. During the twentieth century many museums and universities have similarly been built as the result of open competitions, and in Dublin an entire area of the city.

In Australia, however, few large international competitions have been held. The two notable buildings that have been built from winning designs are the Sydney Opera House, for which Joern Utzon won the competition in 1957, and the new Federal Parliament House in Canberra, won by Mitchell/Giurgola and Thorp in 1980. It was therefore a surprise when the then Premier of Victoria, Jeff Kennett, announced in 1996 that Federation Square would be built as the result of an international architectural competition.

The site had been earmarked by the government in June 1994, when Mr Kennett nominated the area known as Princes Bridge, where the twin Gas and Fuel buildings stood, as Victoria's principal site for development as part of the Centenary of Federation – a place for civic celebrations and for the public to enjoy – the public square that Melbourne had always wanted.

There was a large response to the competition, 177 entries eventually being received, of which 41 were from overseas – including 18 from the UK and 6 from the USA. Lab architecture studio, based in London at the time, produced one of the five plans shortlisted at the end of the first stage and, in order to proceed further with the competition, it formed a partnership with Bates Smart, one of Melbourne's most prominent firms of architects.

The judging panel was headed by Professor Neville Quarry, Professor of Architecture at the University of Sydney, and included the internationally renowned architect Daniel Libeskind. At the end of July 1997 Professor Quarry announced that Lab architecture studio's design was 'unanimously and enthusiastically' declared the winner. He emphasised, 'The winning design has the necessary ingredients required for any structure of longevity and memorable greatness – boldness, freedom, invention and excitement.'

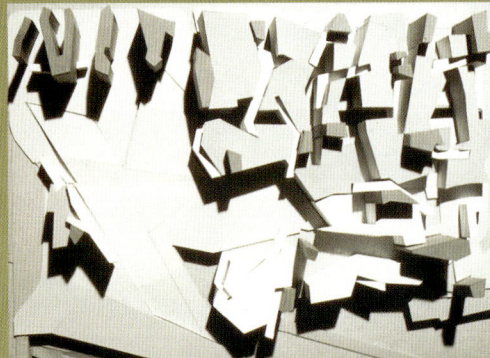

Site model
Stage 1 competition
Lab architecture studio

Presentation model
Lab architecture studio

The international architectural design competition announced by the then Premier Jeff Kennett in 1996 (see page 40) for this site north of Princes Bridge and bounded on one side by Flinders Street and the other side by the Yarra River, was the beginning of Melbourne's Federation Square. The seven-member judging panel, chaired by Professor Neville Quarry, announced that Lab architecture studio (London) and Bates Smart Architects (Melbourne) had won the job and praised their winning design: 'The winning scheme draws its inspiration from the unique urban characteristics of Melbourne's arcades and lanes and transforms these elements into a new form of organisation, celebrating the city'.

'Federation Square is the creation of a new centre of cultural activity for Melbourne – the long-awaited large, open public civic destination. In the true spirit of Federation, the design brings together distinct elements and activities.'

With an architecture of 'difference and coherence' the design has brought together distinct elements and activities while maintaining a visual and formal coherence. The site has also produced a cultural and civic precinct based on permeability – allowing for the interaction of visitors, precinct workers and passersby.

The architects' initial 3.2-hectare Federation Square plan integrated civic spaces, a transport hub, tourist and civic facilities. Buildings and open space defined a precinct stretching from Swanston Street to Melbourne Park, distinguished by a number of features:

- a large irregularly shaped city square (or plaza)
- a plaza to be known as St Paul's Court, facing north and creating a sunny sheltered area for al fresco dining, street theatre and music
- a building complex along the Flinders Street frontage, providing gallery space, performance space and facilities for cafes
- a building complex above and over the Russell Street extension, to house the Cinemedia (now ACMI) centre, multimedia facilities and offices
- a glass 'wintergarden' atrium slicing through the two major building complexes, complete with rainforest and desert greenhouses
- a free-standing restaurant, and a free-standing viewing tower.

Subsequently Federation Square evolved to include a venue to exhibit the National Gallery of Victoria's Australian Art Collection, the adaptation of the originally envisaged 'wintergarden' into a galleria-like structure and indoor amphitheatre and the inclusion of considerably more commercial tenancies and uses, including a function centre.

THE BUILDING OF FEDERATION SQUARE

At the conclusion of the design competition, there was great haste to proceed with the project. The State Government in collaboration with the Commonwealth Government secured an additional $50 million (through the Federation Fund). The Government set ambitious timelines for the project, keen to have the development completed in time for 9 May 2001, the date that marks one hundred years of Australian nationhood and the official Centenary of Federation. To meet this timeline, the project needed to be 'fast-tracked'.

The pressure to fast-track construction of the Square meant that the structural deck over the Jolimont rail yards began before the plans were completed and the design became by necessity a design of emergence allowing for change and the evolution of the site. It also proved particularly difficult for the designers, engineers and builders as they had little time to plan anything in advance of actual construction.

The construction of the railway deck (see page 43) commenced the second stage of Federation Square, with the first stage being the rationalisation of the railway lines. A major consideration in the building of the deck was flexibility as much of what was to be built above the deck was at that stage still unknown.

There was, in fact, a major change announced soon after construction had actually commenced. The State Government with the National Gallery of Victoria resolved to split the NGV into two campuses – with its international collection to be exhibited at a refurbished gallery site on St Kilda Road, and a specialist Australian gallery to be developed as part of Federation Square. This necessitated the architects and engineers to restructure their plans for the entire site.

In the late 1990s, Multiplex Constructions were awarded the contract to construct Federation Square (on top of the 'sub-structure' that had been built by Leighton Constructions) by the then Office of Major Projects acting on behalf of the State Government. This involved major contractual complexities as the State Government was not yet in a position to receive a 'fixed' price from Multiplex, because the design work was not complete. Initially, it was intended that the contract be 'novated', that is moved to a fixed price contract sometime after works commenced. However, this never eventuated because there was never the view that the project was sufficiently well-advanced in a design sense to get a reasonable fixed price from the contractors.

Construction of the Deck

Federation Square's location is at one of Melbourne's busiest intersections, with an estimated 63 million visitations each year (source: Arup Transportation Planning, 2000). It is also the location of the Jolimont Rail Yards – a crucial rail hub through which scores of trains each day ferry hundreds of thousands of passengers to and from the city. Amazingly, Federation Square was to be built on a deck over the top of the rail yards.

The construction of the deck beneath the Square is understood to be the largest expanse of railway decking ever built in Australia. This was a particularly ambitious undertaking that took some twelve months to complete. The building process also had some unusual circumstances. Because normal train operations were to continue, structural work was only permitted in the early hours of the morning when normal train operations had temporarily ceased. So building could only go on for a limited time each day and usually it was in the dark. An overhead electrical traction system, like that under Federation Square, constitutes an unforgiving environment from a safety and logistics point of view.

The deck is supported by over 3,000 tonnes of steel beams, 1.4 kilometres of concrete 'crash walls' and over 4,000 vibration-absorbing spring coils and rubber padding. The deck is designed to support some of the most sensitive uses imaginable – galleries, cinemas, and radio and television studios – and it needed to isolate them from vibration and noise.

If the location and its uses were the major complicating factors for the project's success, they were also one of its most important assets in terms of public benefit. The first of these benefits has as much to do with what was replaced as with what was built. For decades the Jolimont Rail Yards have been an unsightly scar on the face of central Melbourne, cutting it off from one of its great and, until recently, unrealised assets, the Yarra River.

Removing the rail yards and linking the central business district with the Yarra River was a dream that emerged repeatedly over the past one hundred years, but due to engineering complexities and other factors had never become reality. The design and engineering innovation of Federation Square has now seen this dream realised.

Photos: Federation Square Management

Photos: Federation Square Management

In mid-1999 the State Government set up the Federation Square Management Company with the charter to own and operate the Square on its behalf. In September 1999, State Government elections were held, resulting in what most at the time would agree was the surprise demise of the Kennett Liberal Government, and the election of the Labor Government led by Steve Bracks. While there had been uneasy relationships between the project and the Labor Government while in opposition, the new State Government resolved early to support the project and to see it through to completion.

The Federation Square Management Company, in conjunction with the State Government in early 2000, appointed a Chief Executive, Peter Seamer, who commenced the task of building an organisation to undertake the operational and commercial activities of the Square, assume responsibilities as client for the project, and tackle what had by then become a poor media and public perception towards the project and its implications for Melbourne.

At the request of the State Government in late 2000, Federation Square Management submitted a report on progress of construction, which led to the Government requesting Federation Square Management take over the construction responsibilities of the project from the then Office of Major Projects. Federation Square Management asserted a restructured management regime to the project.

Federation Square Management, with the architects (Lab + Bates Smart), project managers (Clifton Coney Stevens) and managing contractors (Multiplex), progressed with the task of completing the project in the face of a variety of challenges.

The Premier of Victoria, the Hon. Steve Bracks, MP, officially opened Federation Square on Saturday 26 October 2002.

Federation Square was an enormous undertaking and a challenge of immense proportion, not just because of the scale and cost of the project, but also because of its complexity, its diversity of features, its topical and at times politicised nature as well as the logistics of managing such a large scale project in such a central location.

THE NEW CENTRE OF MELBOURNE

Since opening, Federation Square has been embraced by locals and visitors alike. It has attracted twice the number of local and international visitors anticipated; it has become both the gateway and focus that the early proposals aspired to but could never achieve; and it has been awarded Victoria's, Australia's and a number of the world's most prestigious architectural and engineering awards.

Visitor numbers have exceeded even the most optimistic forecasts, almost doubling early predictions commissioned from KPMG. Federation Square is attracting over 6 million visits per annum. Already half the visitors are from outside of Melbourne, alerting Melbourne businesses to the drawcard the Square has become for interstate and overseas visitors.

A key feature of Federation Square now is the sheer volume of activity it hosts. Virtually all the city's major festivals use its unique facilities, and over 1,500 events and activities are held there annually. With these events, its venues and the stunning architecture, Federation Square is the major tourist attraction in Victoria.

Federation Square from Swanston Street
Photo: David Simmonds

The Ian Potter Centre: NGV Australia

The new home for the Australian collection of the National Gallery of Victoria is the Ian Potter Centre. It is situated at the eastern end of Federation Square, and stretches almost the whole block from Flinders Street down to the Yarra River walk. The exterior of the Ian Potter Centre is clad in the triangular fractal facade that is so striking a feature of Federation Square, where sandstone, zinc and glass come together in a vast abstract work of art.

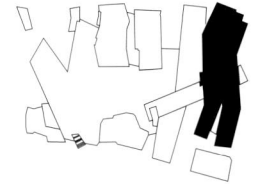

The gallery is designed as two north–south 'filaments', which form an angular and elongated figure of eight. The main entrance to the gallery and access to the three levels of the building are positioned where the two filaments meet, at the Crossbar; stairs, escalators and lifts are all accessed here, and 'vertical movement becomes part of the building's internal drama', according to Lab architecture studio. The floor of this area is the Kimberley sandstone that paves the square, creating a visual link with the rest of the precinct.

Between the two filaments are intra-filamentary spaces. The architects designed them to be 'an important spatial reference, assisting in providing location within the building. These spaces are both of rest and refreshment, with internal and external views and multimedia facilities to allow greater enquiry into the collections'. The soaring volumes of the intra-filamentary spaces allow crossings between the strands of the building. The space between the northern strands is more enclosed and darker than the southern space, which has views opening on to the Yarra River and the riverside walk through a folded glass wall. For the visitor, the figure-eight layout means one can wander through the galleries in a coherent pattern, but the intra-filamentary spaces allow glimpses of adjoining rooms and their contents, and the opportunity to move between the filaments rather than adhere to the figure-eight composition in a strict way.

Other elements of the architecture catch the eye of a visitor: for instance, the wooden stairs that rise from the ground floor up to the higher levels are spectacular, while the ironbark timber flooring is golden, warm and welcoming, with horizontal slatting as part of the heating and cooling system that is a work of art in itself. Even the ceilings of the galleries are unusual: odd slashes of shapes to allow recessed lighting.

The National Gallery of Victoria has a large collection of Australian art: over 20,000 works. Despite its size this large new building displays only a fraction of the collection, but there is space for about 850 works to be on view over the three levels. The artworks on show are rotated regularly, to allow as many as possible to be seen.

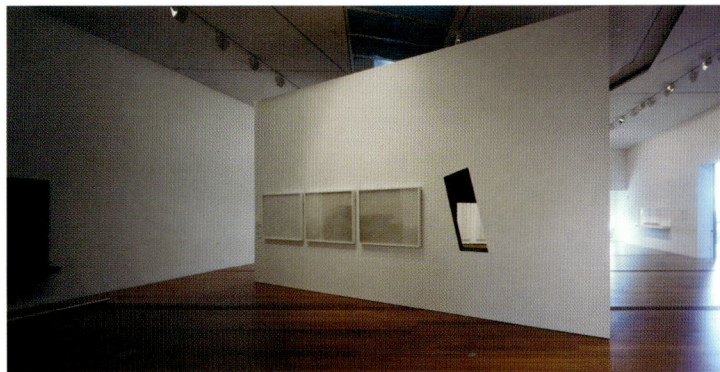

Level 3, Gallery 19: Temporary Exhibitions

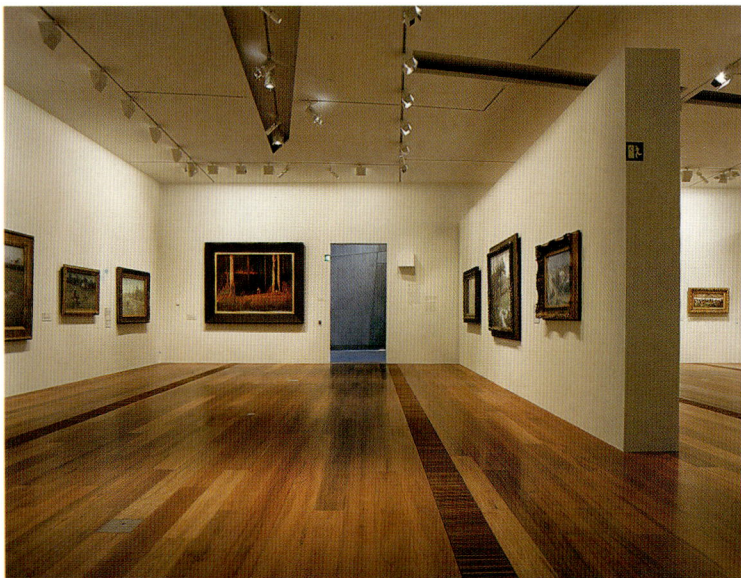

Level 2, Gallery 6: Colonial to Heidelberg

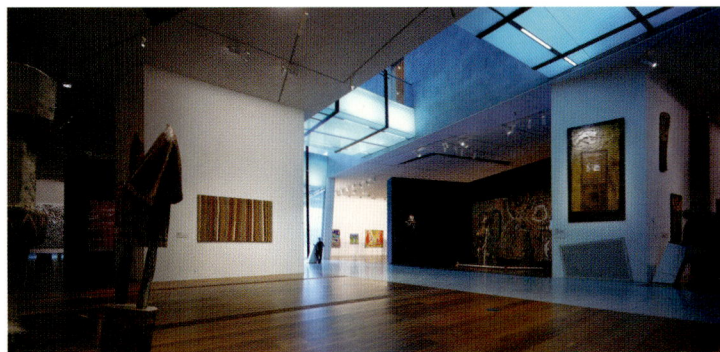

Level G, Gallery 2: Aboriginal & Torres Strait Islander

Level 3, Gallery 18: Temporary Exhibitions

The ground floor of the gallery contains a theatrette, the NGV Response Gallery facing on to Flinders and Russell streets, designed to stage exhibitions focusing on Melbourne and the community, and the NGV's collection of indigenous art, both Aboriginal and Torres Strait Islander. Here many media are displayed: from bark paintings and paintings on canvas to sculpture, from weaving to photography. Internationally renowned artists such as Emily Kam Kngwarray, Ginger Riley, Rover Thomas and Lin Onus are represented, but there has also been an effort to show work from Aboriginal communities around Australia. The Pukumani (funeral ceremony) works from the Tiwi islands north of Darwin include bark paintings and carved and painted poles, while there is a wonderful selection of Dreaming paintings from the Western Desert. Emily Kam Kngwarray's vast *Big Yam Dreaming* is a spectacular canvas, while Lin Onus's *Fish* looks non-indigenous in concept and execution, until one realises that the fish swimming through the current are all decorated with 'rarrk', cross-hatched Aboriginal designs.

The floor above, Level Two, contains the permanent collection of nineteenth- and twentieth-century Australian art, arranged chronologically. Classic favourites such as Tom Roberts's iconic *Shearing the Rams* and Frederick McCubbin's *The Pioneer*, that poignant triptych depicting the travails of a pioneering family's life, now hang here; John Brack's *Collins Street 5 p.m.* is next to his arresting self-portrait, a relatively recent acquisition; Rupert Bunny and E. Phillips Fox, Fred Williams and Sidney Nolan, Margaret Preston and Grace Cossington Smith, Albert Tucker and Arthur Boyd, are all well represented, while the powerful work of modern artists such as Peter Booth is also to be found. One room is designated for Contemporary Projects: regularly changing exhibitions of the latest work from Australia's leading contemporary artists, which may be installations or based on multi-media.

Level Three is principally for temporary exhibitions. These may be major retrospectives of one artist, or surveys of a theme. Temporary exhibitions are also drawn from the NGV's collections of photography, prints, fashion and textiles, and drawings and contemporary art.

Level 3, Gallery 18 looking through central structure to south wall exhibit.

Foyer looking to skylight

Foyer

ACMI
AUSTRALIAN CENTRE FOR THE MOVING IMAGE

The Australian Centre for the Moving Image is dedicated to preserving the moving image in all its forms, from the earliest silent films to the very latest digital technology, interactive exhibits and video art installations. At Federation Square, along Flinders Street, two large buildings are joined by a glass central arcade: together these make the Alfred Deakin Building, the homes of ACMI and SBS, Australia's national multicultural television, radio and on-line broadcaster.

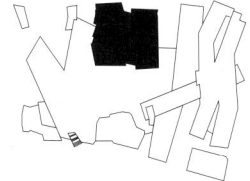

The facade is covered with the wonderful fractal patterning that is so arresting to the passer by. However, the eastern half of the Alfred Deakin Building is almost windowless – it houses two cinemas – and thus the facade is almost entirely of sandstone and zinc, in contrast to the western half, where more glass appears. Although a whole, the two parts of the building are delineated by their differing cladding.

The arcade between the two parts of ACMI leads from Flinders Street into the Square. Its glass ceiling throws light into the centre, and allows the arcade also to function as a foyer for the eastern and western elements. It was designed by Lab architecture studio to link 'the main elements, providing the primary street and plaza entry, as well as forming the main foyer and circulation spaces which vertically connect all the functional components. At the ground level, both buildings are joined by the arcade foyer and its linkage of the ticketing, educational and retail areas.'

As one walks through the building one is constantly reminded of its purpose: large screens show exhibits of moving art, while small screen lounges with plasma screens allow visitors to view videos. The technology behind the surface is state-of-the-art. The building is networked with extensive fibre optic cables and switches, on a scale never before seen. One electronic system controls all that goes on, from media streaming and film projection to video games and the production suites.

The cinemas are intended for film festivals and special presentations that are extremely high tech in nature. The larger cinema holds 400 people and is capable of showing films from wide 70 millimetre format down to 16 millimetre, while the smaller, 200-seat cinema can show films from 35 millimetre format to Super-8. The technological wizardry is not confined to the projection systems, however, as when the lights dim in the cinemas a magical spatial effect is created by lighting through the walls.

As well as showing films, ACMI runs a lending library for members. The Lending Collection was established in 1946, and it is Australia's largest, consisting of more than 35,000 items: films, videos, CD ROMs and DVDs. Whether you are interested in feature films or shorts, student films or foreign language films, ACMI has something for everyone.

ACMI is also focused on bringing film-making to as wide an audience as possible. With this in mind, the western building houses a web-casting studio, a video production lab for digital filming, sound work, animation and editing, an electronic classroom and an interactive media research library, all of which are available to the public.

The western half of the Alfred Deakin Building houses the administration of ACMI and the Melbourne headquarters of SBS – the Special Broadcasting Service and 'the voice and vision of multicultural Australia'. SBS broadcasts in over 60 languages, on radio and television, and its television programs are watched by more than 50 per cent of Australian households each week. The Alfred Deakin Building contains SBS studios for radio, television and new multi-media.

Finally, below ground on the Flinders Street side of the Square and running parallel to the railway lines, there is a cavernous space, ACMI's Screen Gallery, for screen-based exhibitions.

ACMI cinema 01

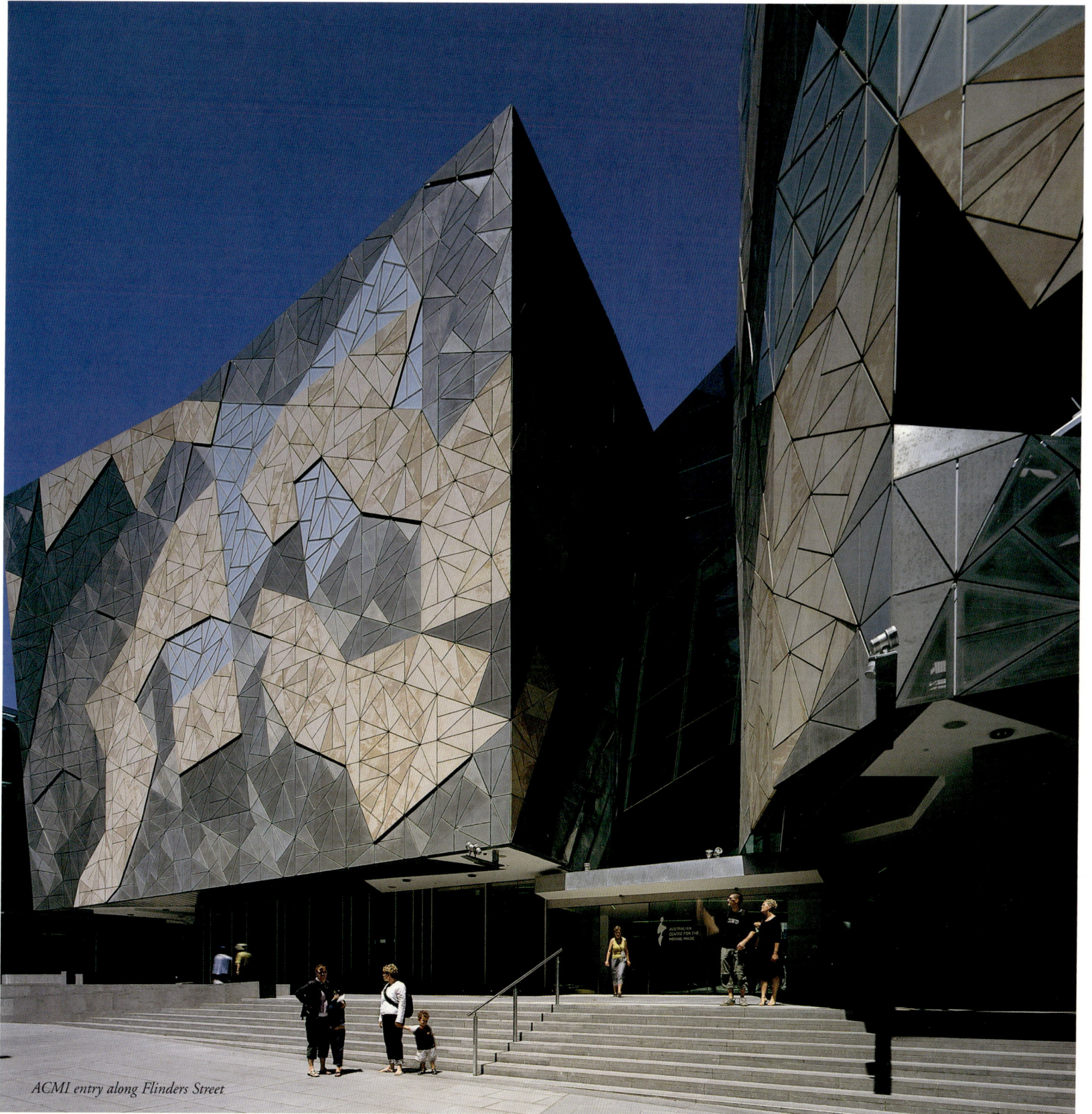

ACMI entry along Flinders Street

ACMI theatre, wall detail

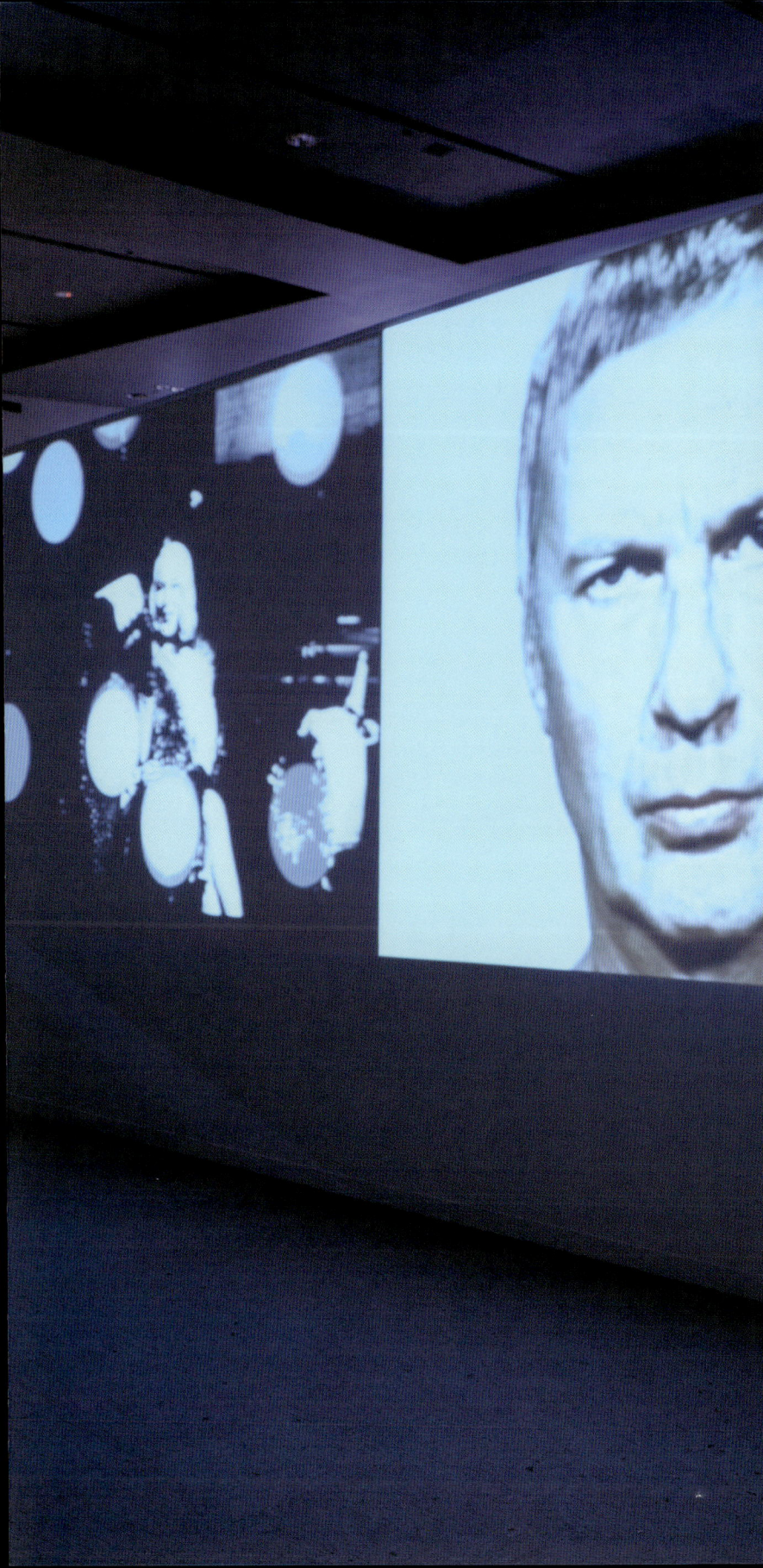

Screen Gallery

The Screen Gallery runs underground parallel to Flinders Street and has been built in the space that once contained two platforms of the former Princes Bridge railway station. Reached by a wide flight of stairs from the foyer of the Australian Centre for the Moving Image, it is a dark and mysterious space to enter. The darkness is unavoidable: because many of the exhibits are fragile, flickering images, the visitor's concentration must be held on each in turn, and not be overwhelmed by the surroundings, or nearby exhibits.

The Screen Gallery is 110 metres long, 15 metres wide and 8 metres high – a truly vast space. It is designed to be as flexible as possible. To this end, there is a huge steel mezzanine floor which is retractable, allowing the Screen Gallery to have varying flooring configurations. Within the space 'rooms' can be built to isolate particular exhibits that require total separation for their effects to work most powerfully.

The Screen Gallery is home to temporary exhibitions. What you may find here can range from showings of classic films to interactive installations, from video artwork to computer graphics creations. Many of these are challenging and powerful views of the world from perspectives not generally encountered. When the visitor rises from the shadows of the Screen Gallery back into the foyer of ACMI he or she will have much to reflect on.

ACMI Screen Gallery

ACMI incorporates some extremely sensitive functions, such as recording studios and cinemas.
Most of Federation Square was built on a deck with springs at its base, to insulate the
buildings from vibration and noise from the trains.
There are more than 4,000 spring coils and rubber pads to help with this insulation.

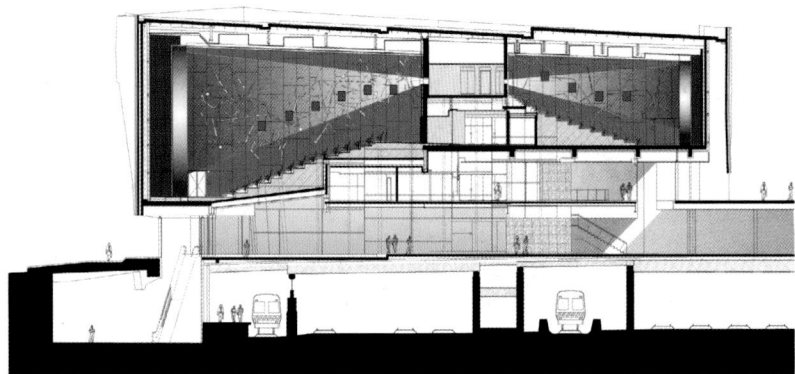

ACMI section through cinemas looking east
Lab architecture studio

ACMI Screen Gallery stairs
with Emily Weil's Platform 1 on the
screen in the background

ACMI central arcade view to south

THE SQUARE

The main focus of the architectural competition to design Federation Square was a square that would accommodate up to 15,000 people at one time, along with associated cultural and commercial buildings. Melbourne has long lacked a civic centre where people could assemble, and although there is an open area off Swanston Street known as the City Square, it has never been popular with Melburnians and is too small to hold large gatherings. Thus there was a perceived need for a large, striking square, somewhere that offered both space and function: restaurants, bars, an entertainment area … somewhere, in essence, that people would want to spend time wandering through or sitting around, and which would host a large gathering at times of celebration.

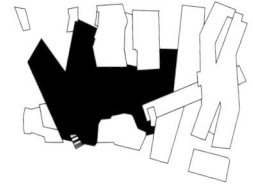

Lab architecture studio was very conscious of the importance of the square in the overall Federation Square development: 'It is a key for the entire project, establishing precise and varying relationships with the acknowledged diverse context of the city and landscape around the site … The design's geometry allows for a vast array of configurations and arrangements, from the largest scale public gathering of up to 15,000 people to intimate sites of relaxation and contemplation.'

The Square gradually rises from street level along Swanston Street until it is about 6 metres higher at the eastern end, near the Atrium and the Ian Potter Centre: NGV Australia. Seen from the street it is attractive: against the grey macadam and the bluestone of surrounding streets and buildings, the Square is like a breath of outback Australia, for it is paved with golden, red, ochre, sandy yellow and occasionally purple sandstone cobbles.

These extraordinary and beautiful cobbles were quarried in Western Australia. The architects had seen a sample of the stone, and were determined to use it; however, the location the sample had come from was not definite. The stone outcrops were finally found in the Kimberley on a four-wheel drive trip, using a geology map and a global positioning system.

A quarry was opened, where the workers had to cope with temperatures reaching 45°C during summer and learned to avoid the basking brown snakes. The raw blocks were trucked out over dirt road on their way to Broome and then on to Perth, where they were split into cobbles.

Australia Day 2004
Photo: John Gollings

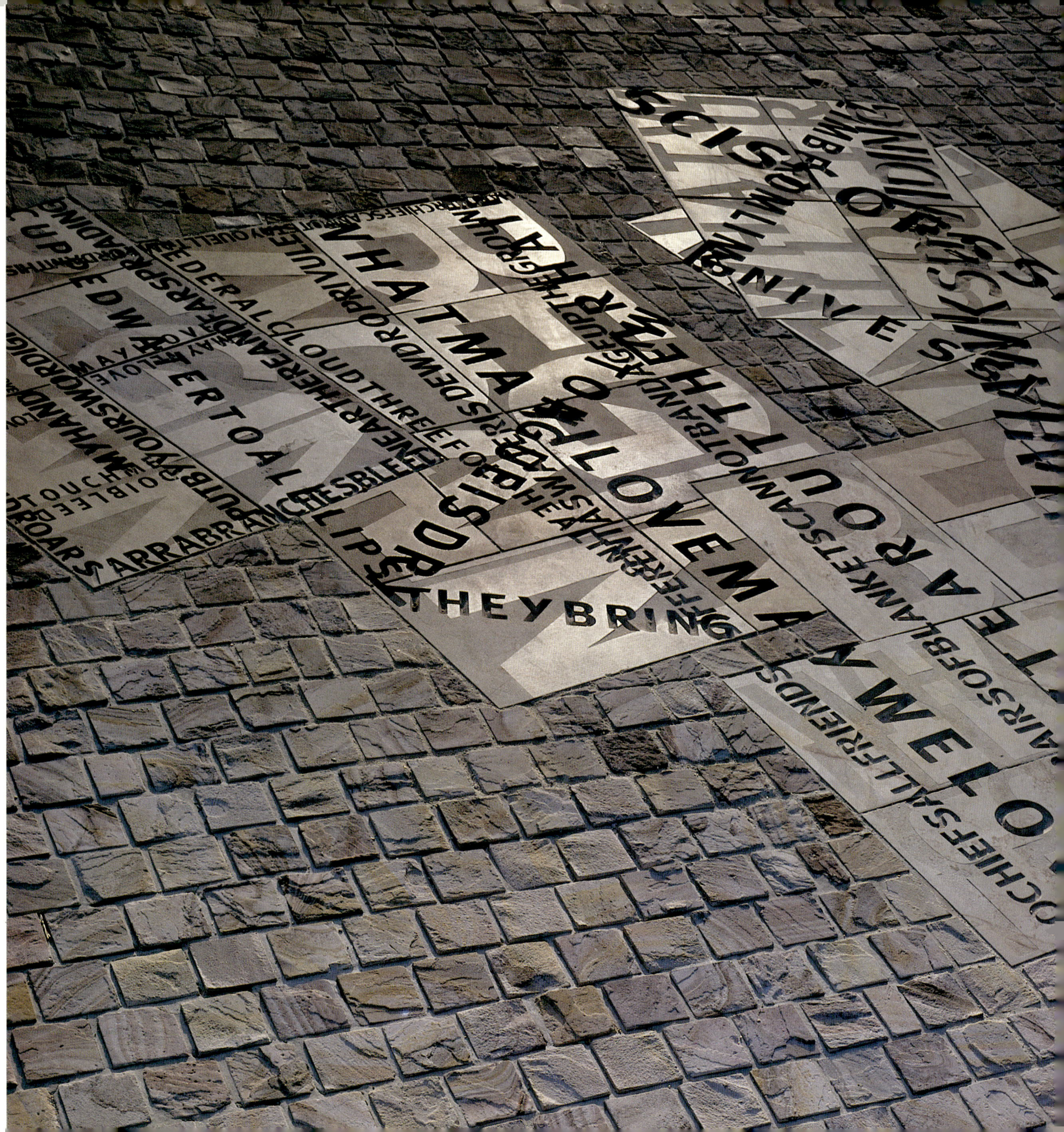
THEYBRING

Paul Carter's Square Artwork: *Nearamnew*

Nearamnew is a pidgin word, derived from the Aboriginal word 'narr-m', which signifies 'the place where Melbourne now stands'. Paul Carter's *Nearamnew* celebrates the emergence of a new space, and brings together ideas of histories and patterns that are part of the place.

The complex purplish-pink whorl pattern of the cobbles is difficult to appreciate from the ground. Aerial photographs reveal the topography of the design, the whorls radiating from the top of the steps that lead up into the Square from Swanston Street. Paul Carter has suggested that these whorls are in part representative of the billabongs that flooded along the Yarra River, in the area where Federation Square now stands, and in part are modelled on a section of a bark etching that was found at Lake Tyrrell near Swan Hill. The whorls are the memory traces of the place, the ancient past.

As well as the whorls there are nine paved figures set into the cobbles around the Square. Into these figures 'federal poems' have been carved. These are words or phrases associated with the idea of the place, and of the Federation of Australia, which the whole square commemorates. The figures are the expression of many histories stemming from this place, while the fragmentary nature of them gives an elusive quality to the whole. The work has been described as 'a cryptic encyclopedia in stone: a ground design that marks the site as a federated place, as a distribution of meeting places, desire lines and accumulated memories'.

There was extraordinary attention to detail in creating *Nearamnew*. For instance, the font in which the texts are carved was designed specially for this artwork, and has been named Federal. The words are carved into the stone at three different levels, a reflection of the peculiar way in which memories work: some are deeper and more lasting than others.

Relief plan of Nearamnew artwork No. 5
Lab architecture studio

Events at Federation Square

Parades and public gatherings in Melbourne were traditionally confined to main streets and the steps of civic buildings. Federation Square now provides the city with a cultural and civic precinct that gives Melburnians and event organisers a central location and communal space for everything from New Year's Eve celebrations, AFL Grand Finals, Spring Racing Carnival Parades to demonstrations.

The Square was purpose-designed and built to provide a public space where people could meet, a landmark for visitors, for spontaneous celebrations, parades and public events. Its versatile, sloping topography offers space for outdoor performances and activities and, through its large video screen, a public forum for launches, promotions and sporting and cultural 'live site' gatherings.

The Atrium is an adaptive inspirational space for arts, roving performances, temporary exhibitions, functions and late evening parties.

The 450-seat indoor amphitheatre, the BMW Edge, at the southern end of the Atrium, with its backdrop views overlooking the river, is a venue for ensemble music, launches, comedy, radio and television broadcasts, cabaret, theatre and public lectures.

Federation Square provides Melbourne with a focus for its busy calendar of festivals, events and promotional activities, and is already becoming our much needed city square.

New Year's Eve 2002
Photo: Peter Clarke

THE FACADE

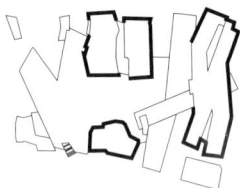

The facade that covers three large buildings in Federation Square – the Alfred Deakin Building, the Ian Potter Centre: NGV Australia and the Yarra Building – is unique, quite unlike anything else in the world. It works as a unified whole, while being substantially different for each element of the project. It is complex and three-dimensional, yet is produced from repetitive triangles. The architects were aiming for site coherence, while ensuring each building was different. The overall impression is one of dynamic movement.

When the Sydney Opera House was built in the 1960s, its roof was the subject of much discussion. Joern Utzon, the Opera House's architect, used two types of tiles, glazed and matt, which together produce a glorious effect when the sun strikes the roof: the glazed tiles glow with immense radiance, while the matt ones do not. At Federation Square, the architects moved beyond this idea into another realm: three materials – glass, zinc and sandstone – have been cut into identical shapes, but are then put together in a way that is free-flowing, and works like an abstract sculpture.

The three elements have been carefully chosen. The sandstone triangles are a material reflection of the sandstone cobbles of the Square. Some are rough to touch, while others are smooth. The zinc is used in two ways, as perforated and solid sheets; over the years the now-silvery zinc will (naturally) oxidise and become similar to the dullish blue that is so familiar throughout Melbourne, with its bluestone churches and streets. The glass fulfils dual functions, being part of the facade sculpture at the same time as being a traditional method of illuminating the interiors of the buildings. Some of the glass is opaque, while other triangles are clear.

Each of these three structural elements reacts differently to the weather, becoming relatively brighter or duller compared with each other as the sun shines or the rain falls. Thus each view of the facade will be a slowly changing kaleidoscopic experience, and the facade itself should be seen as a fluid expression of Melbourne's ever-changing weather.

The facade also wraps itself around the buildings. The patterns of the triangles turn the corners, enclosing the interiors; in addition, there are places on each building where the pattern has been folded into itself. When the layout is seen unwrapped and unfolded, on a flat plane, it becomes clear that each building has been designed as a coherent whole, an enormous abstract artwork.

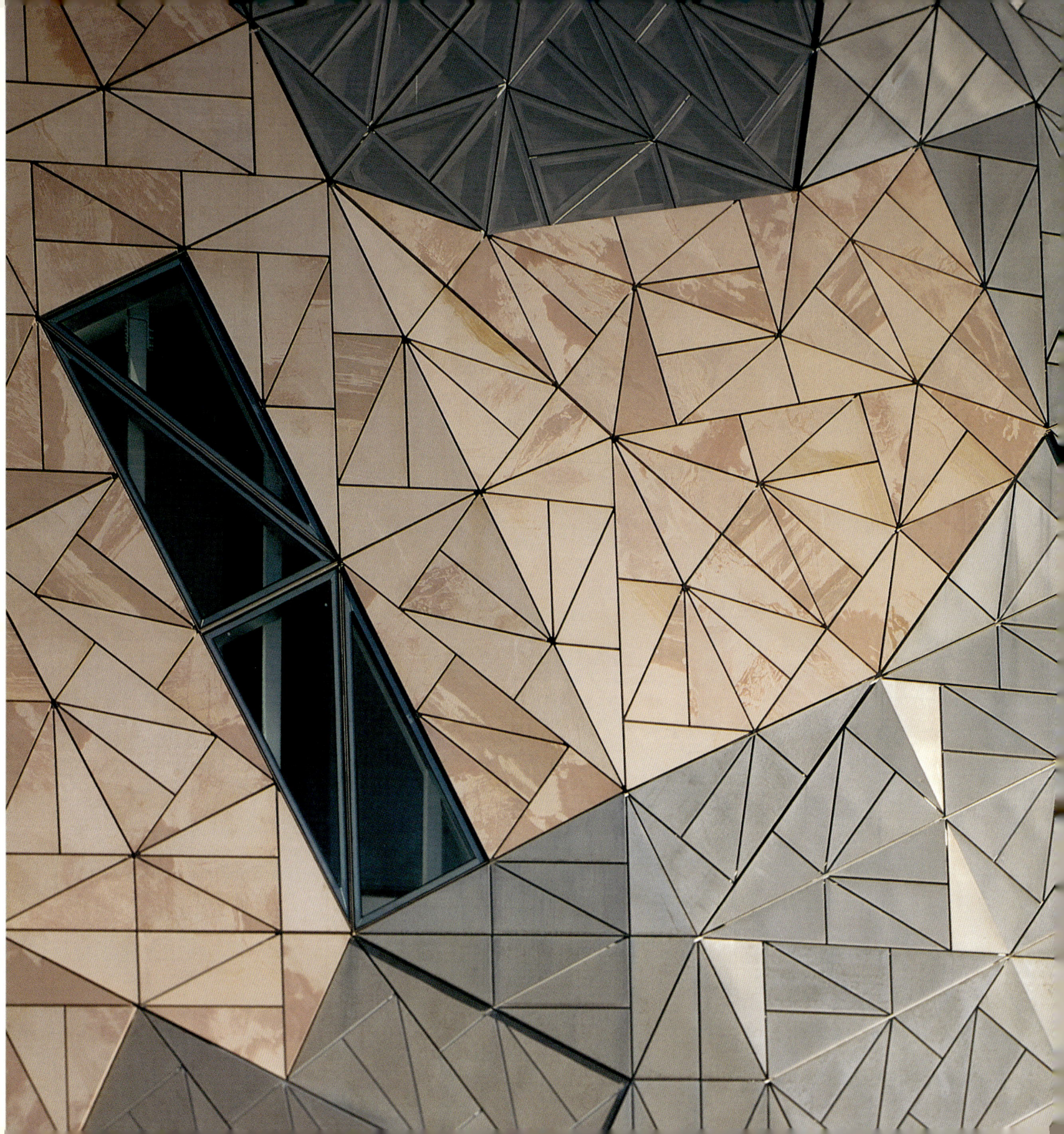

22,073 triangular tiles make up the distinctive external triangular facades of Federation Square.
Of these, there are 7,865 sandstone tiles, 12,325 zinc tiles and 1,883 glass tiles.
600 tonnes of structural steel were used in the facade, in the forms of mullions and grillage.

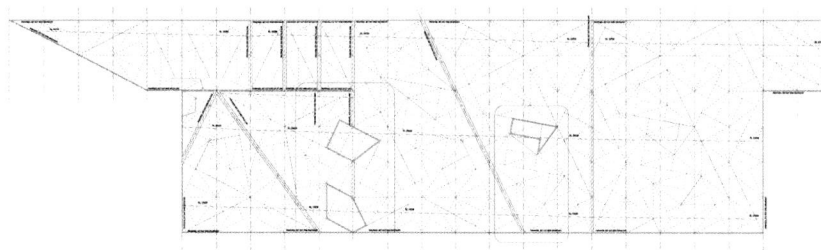

The Ian Potter Centre: NGV Australia
North east filament facade unwrap, showing fold lines
Lab architecture studio

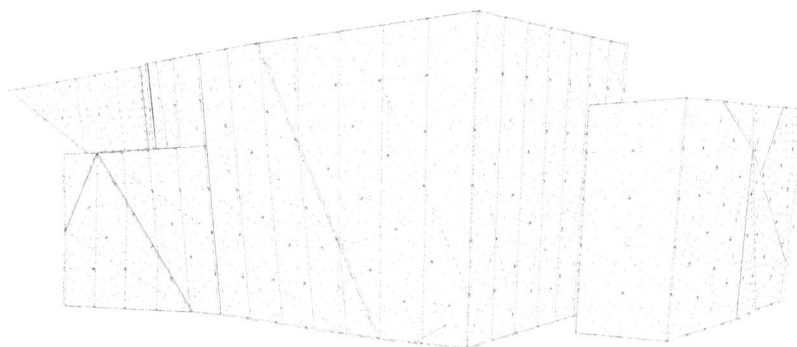

THE ATRIUM

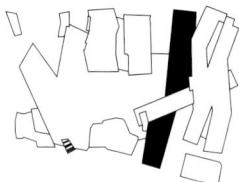

The Atrium runs north–south from Flinders Street to the Yarra River walk, immediately to the west of the Ian Potter Centre: NGV Australia. It is essentially a covered street constructed from glass and steel, and is a feature entry point into Federation Square from Flinders Street. The architects' intention is that the Atrium 'as a continuously open, publicly accessible space … is emblematic of Federation Square's intended connection of city and river'.

To describe it as a covered street does not explain it adequately. It is a vast space, almost cathedral-like, with walls where steel girders are joined in a lace-like mix of complexity and apparent randomness, with glazing between them. It looks as if it should not be standing without more structural support, but it does. In fact, tonnes of galvanised steel were assembled on site to form a perimeter, double-skin wall, the two parts a metre or more apart. It was then glazed externally and internally with a mixture of single and double glazing.

By day the Atrium may be intriguing, but at night it is even more spectacular: it is lit in such a way that the steel reflects the light and turns into a dazzling array of coloured girders that seem to hang in space, defying gravity.

The original starting point for the Atrium's design was the triangular pinwheel geometry of the facade, but it evolved as it was developed into a three-dimensional, folded design. The thick space of the supporting frame works as a thermal chimney: sunlight hits the outer glass layer, the air inside the steel-and-glass frame heats up and rises, being vented at the top of the Atrium. The heating effect of the sun is therefore much reduced on the interior of the space. Cool air is circulated into the Atrium from the Labyrinth via wooden slats in the floor and the Atrium can be up to 12°C cooler than the outside temperature in summer. The temperature control of the Atrium is thus state-of-the-art and mostly passive, and consumes far less energy than ubiquitous air conditioning systems.

North end of Atrium
Photo: Peter Clarke

The BMW Edge, looking south towards Yarra River
Photo: Ian McKenzie

Atrium looking north towards Flinders Street

At the north end a large entrance links Flinders Street with the Atrium. In this northern part of the space the glass rises to 16 metres and the Atrium is up to 20 metres across. On the east side lies the Ian Potter Centre: NGV Australia, and at street level there are retail outlets associated with it. Up to a thousand people can move in the Atrium at any one time.

Two-thirds of the way down the Atrium is the 'Crossbar'. This is a building set at an angle to both the Ian Potter Centre: NGV Australia and the Atrium, slicing through them, as it were. The Crossbar acts as an entry point to the gallery, joining it at the area where the figure-of-eight of its wings cross; here people can also move between the Atrium and the main Square.

South of the Crossbar and once past the railway lines that lie deep beneath the surface, a series of steps leads the Atrium down to a lower ground level. At the southern end of the Atrium, with views through the glass walls to the Yarra River, lies the BMW Edge. This is an indoor amphitheatre designed for music and public theatre; during the building of Federation Square it was acoustically tuned to be suitable for medium-sized theatrical performances and musical ensembles, for example chamber music. It can seat up to 450 people and its fit-out was made possible through the support of BMW Australia.

Nine different shapes of glass tiles were used in the Atrium walls.

The north Atrium contains up to 1,300 glass tiles and 3.6 km of steel tubing was used to build it.

The south Atrium (The BMW Edge) contains up to 980 glass tiles and 2.1 km of steel tubing.

2,740 star connectors hold the steel together at joins.

In all, about 3,880 tonnes of steel were used in the construction.

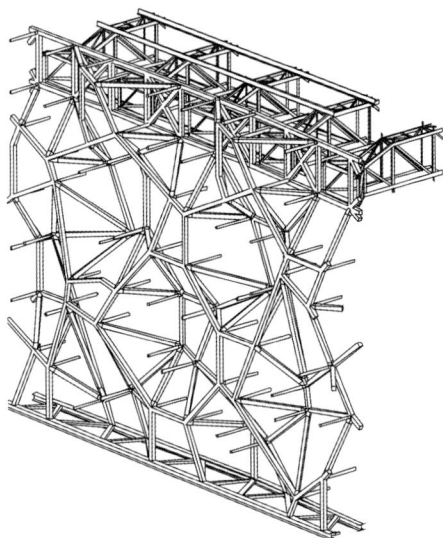

Axonometric of atrium structure
Diagrams: Lab architecture studio

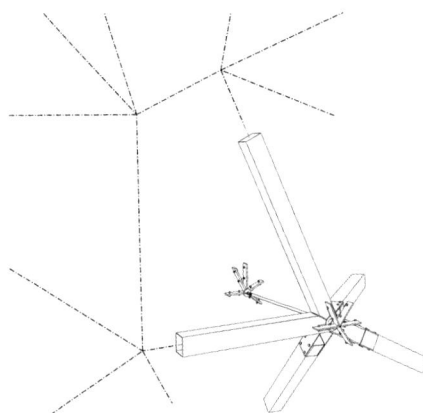

Node detail of atrium structure

The Crossbar

The brief the architects followed for Federation Square demanded a mix of artistic and commercial use around the central Square. The Crossbar is part of the commercial element of Federation Square, while also working as an entry point to the Atrium and the Ian Potter Centre: NGV Australia. It bisects the art gallery, at its eastern end providing an area of public circulation as the foyer for the gallery; the western half of the Crossbar houses a cafe on the ground level and offices and a restaurant above.

The Crossbar is not clad in the fractal facade that distinguishes other buildings in Federation Square. Instead it is covered with dark perforated aluminium. This cladding echoes the outside of Trans*port*, facing it on the western side of the square, where the same material is used, albeit in a different way.

THE LABYRINTH

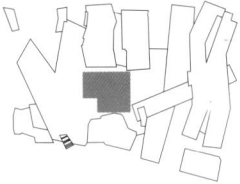

One of the most fascinating aspects of Federation Square is completely hidden: the Labyrinth. It is situated on top of the deck across the railway yards and under the eastern half of the square, where the cobbles slope upwards towards the Atrium. The Labyrinth covers an area of about 160 square metres. The top of the concrete walls of the Labyrinth in fact support the square's deck slab and are a vital part of the square's final surface topography.

It is called the Labyrinth because it resembles a maze. In fact it consists of hundreds of pre-cast concrete walls arranged together like huge interlocking combs, where the teeth are close together but do not touch – they are spaced approximately 60 centimetres apart. The walls (the 'teeth' of the combs) are not flat slabs, but have a zig-zag profile, going in and out. This maximises their surface area.

At night, when the ambient temperature has cooled from daytime highs, the cold outside air is pumped through the Labyrinth's spaces. The concrete slabs cool down and warm exhaust air is extracted. During summer, as day dawns and the sun begins to heat the Atrium, pumping begins again, this time drawing air from the Labyrinth into the Atrium via its floor; the air from the concrete maze is much colder than the temperature in the Atrium and cools that space down. Warm outside air is drawn into the Labyrinth as the Atrium cools, and gradually the concrete maze warms up. It is estimated that the Labyrinth can keep the Atrium up to 12°C cooler than the outside air, which is a result comparable with conventional air conditioning, while using one-tenth of the energy such air conditioning would guzzle and generating less than one-tenth of the carbon dioxide emissions.

If, instead of a hot summer's day, the forecast is for a cooler one, no pumping of cold air into the Labyrinth takes place at night and the concrete walls retain their heat from the day before. The following day warm air can be pumped from the maze into the Atrium and raise its temperature.

The Labyrinth is so efficient at its job of cooling that it is anticipated it will be able to partially cool ACMI when its full capacity is not needed for the Atrium. The energy that has been saved by such an elegant system of passive temperature control is substantial.

Labyrinth walls under construction showing
zigzag prifile which doubles cooling capacity
Photo: Lab architecture studio

Plan of site showing position of labyrinth under the square
Lab architecture studio

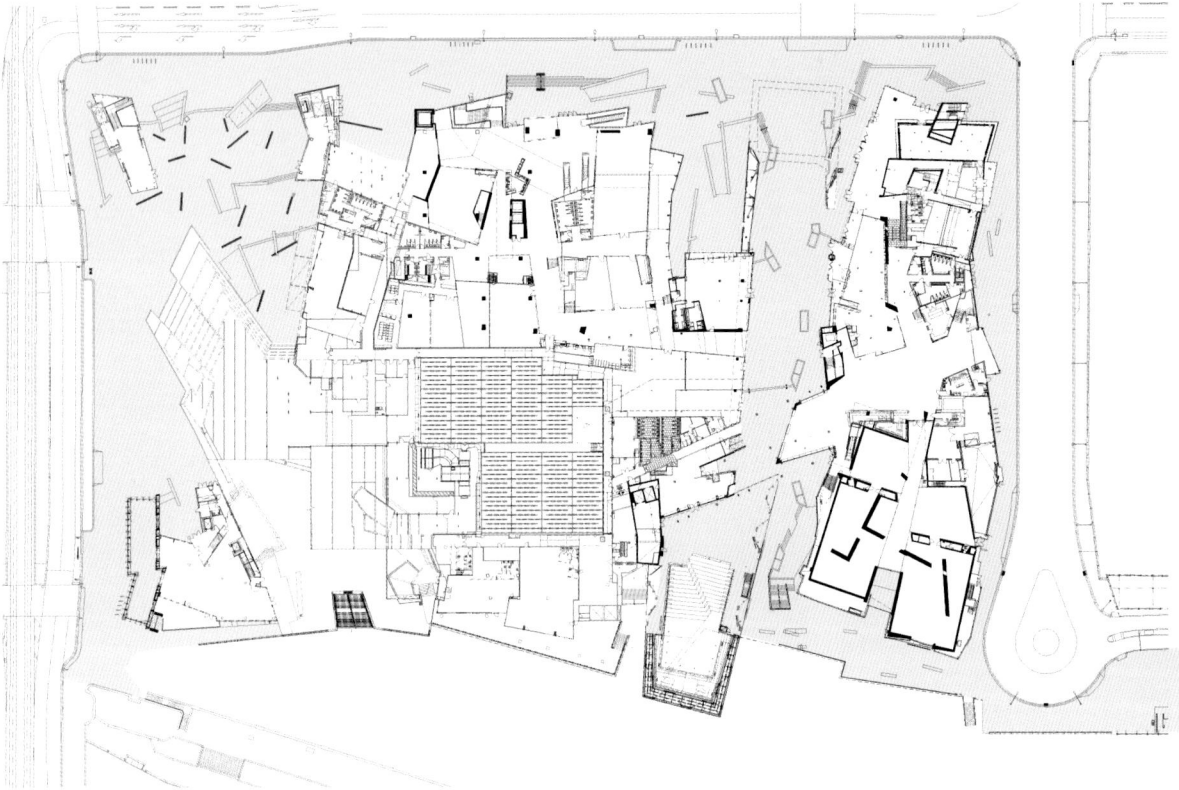

1.2 km of concrete walls were used to construct the Labyrinth
A unique passive cooling system provides environmental climate
control (cooling and heating) for the glazed Atrium

Labyrinth walls
Photo: Lab architecture studio

St Paul's Court
Photo: Peter Clarke

St Paul's Court and the Melbourne Visitor Centre

St Paul's Court is the area of Federation Square directly opposite the twin steeples at the southern end of St Paul's Anglican Cathedral. The cathedral was built in 1880–92, in the Gothic Revival style, and is considered a masterpiece by the English architect William Butterfield; it is elaborately decorated inside and out.

The architects of Federation Square realised the necessity of integrating the cathedral with the new project, and designed the north-west corner of Federation Square with this in mind. The corner of Federation Square opposite St Paul's Cathedral, at Swanston and Flinders streets, is also the most heavily used intersection around the precinct, and therefore is the major gateway for pedestrians into Federation Square.

To ensure the cathedral was not blocked by new structures, St Paul's Court was made an open space of about 30 or 40 metres in width at its border with Flinders Street. At the sides of the court were two 22 metre high buildings that were designed to mirror, as it were, the steeples of the cathedral. These were known as the 'shards' and they now house the Melbourne Visitor (Information) Centre and associated uses. However, the final result was not as envisaged by the architects (see page 103).

Unlike the main Square, St Paul's Court is not paved in sandstone cobbles; instead it is covered by bluestone and concrete pavers. The court's surface rises from the street corner until it leads the visitor into the cobbled area and up a flight of steps into the square. To the east there are commercial and retail outlets. Because of the slope of St Paul's Court, the square itself is not visible until one is almost upon it, and it remains a secret space from the Flinders and Swanston streets intersection.

The eastern 'shard' is a zinc-clad building with a jagged and asymmetric outline. It contrasts with the fractal facade of the adjacent Alfred Deakin Building. As is consistent with the rest of Federation Square, there are no traditional windows in the zinc; rather, there are slits of irregular shape that both act as windows and as a sculpture in the surface of the building, which can be unwrapped to see the whole.

The western building that was originally intended to be a shard at the same height of the eastern shard is now the gateway entrance to the Melbourne Visitor Centre, which serves over 800,000 visitors a year.

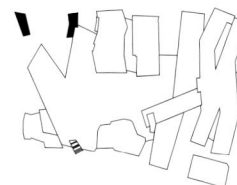

St. Paul's Court looking south
Photo: Peter Clarke

West and south face of western shard

64 million sets of eyes pass through the intersection of Swanston and Flinders streets every year.
It is understood to be the busiest pedestrian intersection in Melbourne.

Looking south from Melbourne Visitor Centre

The Shard Controversy

Lab architecture studio's original concept for the north-western corner of Federation Square involved two similar buildings, the 'shards'. (The term 'shard' was coined by the architects, Peter Davidson and Donald Bates, to describe the largely zinc-clad vertical structures that appear on the site.) Joe Rollo wrote in the *Bulletin*: 'They were meant to act as the key gateway totems into the square and as delicate counterpoints to the eclectic Gothic Revival architecture of St Paul's Cathedral, helping to frame its view, drawing the church in and visually incorporating it as an important element on the edge of the square.'

However, from the time the winning design was announced, debate raged both for and against the design of the most prominent (western) shard proposed for the corner of Swanston and Flinders streets, directly across from Flinders Street Station, Young and Jackson's Hotel and St Paul's Cathedral.

The National Trust and some members of the Melbourne City Council argued to retain the existing vista of St Paul's Cathedral from Princes Bridge, and so in the final design in June 1998 the towers were realigned and reduced in height by 2 metres. In September 1999 the Labor Party narrowly won the state elections which resulted in the Bracks' government putting the shard controversy back on the table. The new Labor government commissioned a review by architect and former Planning Minister Professor Evan Walker in early 2000 which recommended the removal of the three-storey western shard to minimise obstruction to the vista of St Paul's Cathedral from the south. In response, Premier Steve Bracks announced on 17 February 2000 that this predominantly glass shard would be scrapped. The project's architects criticised any removal of the controversial shards, arguing that such intervention would compromise the integrity of their design.

The government's then Project Manager, Damien Bonnice, who was publicly critical of the government's handling of the matter, resigned in March 2000. In June 2000 the Auditor-General reported to Parliament on the project's apparent mismanagement in relation to cost blowouts, the initial judging panel procedures and subsequent decision-making processes.

In October 2000, the State Government announced that the controversial western shard would be replaced by a lower structure, no higher than 8 metres and that it would be the gateway to the new Melbourne Visitor Centre to be built as part of the Square.

The result according to many, is an asymmetrical solution not mirroring the steeples of the cathedral at all and no sooner had Federation Square opened than calls began for the western shard to be rebuilt as originally visualised by the architects.

The development of the western shard has been, and will no doubt remain, contentious, although debate surrounding this feature certainly contributed to the high level of public awareness of the Square.

View looking north at St Paul's Court

Yarra Building: Champions – The Australian Racing Museum and Hall of Fame

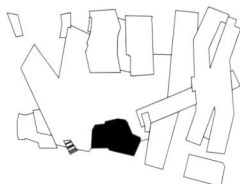

'A square works best if it provides a substantial edge surrounding its multiple paths' wrote Professor Nikos Salingaros – a mathematician and architectural theorist at the University of Texas – in his paper 'Theory of the Urban Web' that appeared in the *Journal of Urban Design*. In other words, a successful square is one that is generally enclosed in some way. The enclosing material may be buildings or, in the case of a natural amphitheatre, rolling landscape. The great squares of the world, such as St Peter's Square in Rome, St Mark's Square in Venice and Trafalgar Square in London, are examples of this.

In order to ensure that Federation Square became a popular venue for Melburnians, it was considered necessary to surround the square with buildings. The Yarra Building encloses the square on its southern side. It is a three-storey building, and therefore has sufficient bulk to visually complete the square. It is not a building that locks people into the square, however; rather, it allows people to move beside it down to the riverside walk.

To keep continuity with the coherent themes of Federation Square, Yarra Building is clad in the fractal facade. However, it looks rather different to the Ian Potter Centre: NGV Australia and the Alfred Deakin Building, more stainless steel grillage – the steel beams and crossbeams under the cladding – being visible than in the rest of Federation Square.

The land around Yarra Building slopes downhill to the river, and on both the eastern and western sides there are several flights of steps leading the pedestrian down. The whole building is designated as commercial spaces, and on both the deck level (towards the river) and the square level there are cafes, restaurants and Champions – The Australian Racing Museum and Hall of Fame. On the riverside face (south) of Yarra Buildings terraces allow views of the river and the swans and boats that glide past: almost opposite Federation Square on the southern bank of the Yarra are a number of large boathouses, and rowers in their sculls, fours or eights are a common – and delightful – sight here.

The facade of the Yarra Building

Transport

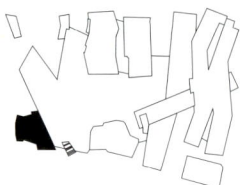

Transport is the name chosen for what originally appeared on plans as Federation Square's 'Neo-Pub'. This building lies at the south-western corner of Federation Square, adjoining Flinders Street and opposite the railway station and Princes Bridge – thus enclosing the square on that side.

Transport is situated at the lower end of the square, and is the focus of many of the sightlines generated by visitors. To capitalise on this, a stage was built on the square side of the building, which when in use turns the square into an amphitheatre. There is also a large video screen above the stage, used for major events, sports 'live sites', promotional and artistic installations.

Although the building has been designed as a pub, it is not a traditional one with dark wooden bars, mirrors and brass. The architects describe it as 'a crystalline volume … embedded into a zinc shard'. The main part of the three-storey building, holding the bars and kitchens, is clad in zinc, and the digital screen is attached to the eastern face of the zinc.

To the south and west of the zinc shard are wide terraces at the second and third level and these are surrounded by a black aluminium, perforated screen. During the day shadows play across the metal screen and patrons inside will be protected both from wind and ultra-violet rays by its shading, but at night light will pour out from the pub through the holes. The design of the neo-pub is intended to be inherently flexible, so that internal spaces can be opened up for ventilation or closed off as required.

The Flinders and Swanston streets intersection has long been famous for one pub, Young and Jackson's, where *Chloe* reigns unadorned. With the arrival of Trans*port,* Melbourne has a very different kind of public house in the area – one for the twenty-first century.

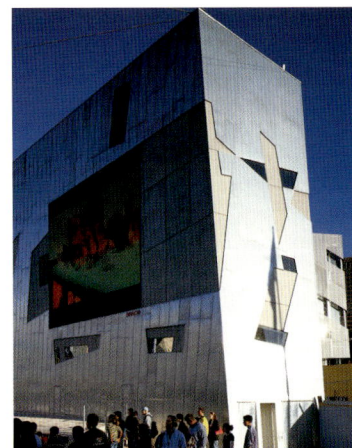

*The 'big screen' situated on the back
wall of the Trans*port *building*

View looking south to Transport Hotel
Photo: Rhiannon Slatter

Exterior and interior of Transport Hotel
Photos above and opposite: Rhiannon Slatter

THE TEAM

Photo: John Donegan

THE MAKERS OF MELBOURNE'S NEW HEART

A large and incredibly diverse number of people were and continue to be involved in the developement of Federation Square and now its operation. It is likely that upwards of 4,000 people have played their direct part from over 300 different companies and countless number of professions and disciplines.

In the early morning of 16 May 2002 a gathering of many of these people (est. 1,400) took place. It was a particularly euphoric event that was captured on film by *The Age* newspaper. It was given front-page billing days later and accompanied by the header: Meet the Makers of Melbourne's New Heart.
This event together with two public 'open days' proved to be a public relations coup that helped turn the tide of support in favour of the project.

Nathan Abate, Jim Adam, Mick Adami, Mel Adams, Rob Adams, Vanessa Adams-Goulding, Ben Albury, Kim Aleksandrowicz, Sam Alexander, Daniel Alie, Kate Allen, Lachlan Allen, Sandra Allen, Tony Allen, Adam Altham, Colin Ambrose, Sofia Anapliotis, Andrew Anastasios, Derek Anderson, Mark Anderson, Steve Andrejic, Athena Andriotis, George Angelakis, Veronica Angelatos, Angelo Angelopoulos, Greg Anton, Tony Antoniou, Daniela Arcieri, Michael Argyrou, Alan Armitt, Katherine Armstrong, Lisa Armstrong, Roger Arnall, Tony Arnel, Peter Arnold, Jeff Arnold, Ian Arrowsmith, Chez Asch, Louise Ashworth, David Asker, Vanitha Athisdam, Megan Atkins, Robert Atkinson, Peter Auman, Peter Axup, Fernando Azevedo, Greg Azzopardi, Al Babicka, Nadia Babicka, Paul Baehr, Tim Bailey, Peter Bain, Brian Baker, Dean Baker, Jaya Balendra, Andrew Balfour, Andrew Ballard, Dragan Banadinovic, Daniela Barbieri, Tony Barbieri, Costa Barboussas, Clare Bardsley, Marc Barfoot, Peter Barnard, Ian Barnes, Rod Barrett, Ken Bartlett, Mark Bartoli, Lisa Barton, Wayne Barwick, Elia Basso, The Hon Minister Peter Batchelor MP, Don Bates, David Batey, Norman Batterham, Ian Bayfield, Robert Beales, Romas Beatty, Diego Beckinschtein, Gunther Behrendt, Leo Belci, Dante Belia, Guiseppe Belia, Chris Bell, David Bell, Rod Bennett, Rob Bergers, Andrew Bernadou, Tiffany Bernard, Ken Bernard, Robert Beveridge, Matt Beveridge, Peter Bickle, Brendan Bishop, Colin Bishop, Geoff Bishop, Yehudi Blacher, Russell Black, Dean Blackley, William Blakeney, Malcolm Blaylock, Elly Bloom, Janine Bofill, Peter Bohret, Chantal Boisgontier, Michael Boland, Dominic Bonadio, Simone Bonella, Andre Bonnice, Damien Bonnice, Silvano Bonotto, Dominic Borello, Francine Borg, David Borthwick, John Bortoli, Sean Boston, Matthew Boulton, Rima Boumadi, Mark Boxshall, David Boyd, Garth Bradbury, Colleen Brady, Kate Brady, Andrew Brain, Iain Bramley, Adam Brancatisano, Peter Brancatisano, Bart Brands, Libro Bratovic, Peter Braun, Greg Bray, Richard Brenchley, Kate Brennan, Steve Brennan, Pat Broadhurst, Rodney Brooker, Richard Brooks, Shane Browitt, Chris Brown, Geoff Brown, Peter Brown, Peter Bruce, Robert Bruce, Ian Buchanan-Black, Neil Buckley, Nicholas Bufe, Professor Catherin Bull, Bruce Bullard, Terry Bullard, Annie Bunting, Deborah Burdett, Terry Burke, David Burlovic, Rob Burns, Mark Burns, Brian Burton, Brett Butler, Mike Buttery, Paul Byrne-Jones, Paul Byrne-Jones Snr, Raymond Byron, Steve Cain, Ignatius Calderone, Jerry Callaghan, Susie Callil, Tony Callipari, Darren Camilleri, Anna Canji, Arthur Cann, Richard Cann, Wally Caoduro, Peter Cargill, Lisa Carlon, Chris Carlos, Alexandra Carlos, Dennis Carmody, Sergio Carneiro, Marc Carney, Mark Carocci, David Carroll, Peter Carroll, Peter Carroll, Dave Carruthers, Paul Carter, Manny Casaccio, John Catala, Ray Cato, Troy Cavanagh, Cynthia Ceccato, Sarah Chamberlin, Cr Kevin Chamberlin, Roger Chapman, Weng Chan, Rinesh Chand, Bill Chandler, Angela Chang, Scott Chapman, Phillip Charlton, Brant Charman, Glenn Chase, Valerie Cheong, Wayne Chequer, Ray Cheung, Vincent Choi, Slav Chrusiel, Mark Clark, Stuart Clark, Ken Clarke, James Clausen, Lee Cleghorn, Peter Clemenger, Jeff Clifton, Norm Clyne, Joe Coccomello, Michael Coenan, Lynda Colahan, Peter Cole, Peter Coleman, Paul Comrie, Michael Connoley, Ovi Constantin, Con Constantino, Dennis Cook, Roger Coombes, Robbie Cooper, Sarah Cope, John Cordialos, Barry Cordner, John Corgliano, Georgie Corke, Russell Cormack, Mark Cornell, Felicia Corso, Tony Cosma, Doug Cotterell, Adrian Coulter, Jim Cousins, Mat Cox, Terry Crabtree, Bruce Cremin, Charlotte Crichton, Greg Crichton, Tony Croagh, Victoria Crombie, Isobel Crombie, Gary Cropley, Emma Cross, Helen Crossley, Michael Cullen, Andrew Cummings, Bruce Cummings, Mark Cummings, Kerry Cummins, Kevin Cunningham, Travis Cunningham, Veryan Curnow, Mick Cuthbert, Manuel Da Cunha, Serena D'Alessandro, Laurie Dalli, Simon Dalli, Romeo D'Amato, Lauren Dando, Graham Daniel, Luciano Daniele, Ross Darlington, Barry Davidson, John Davidson, Peter Davidson, Troy Davidson, Stephen Davies, Peter Davies, Charlie Davis, Emma Dawson, Geraldine de Fina, Rob De Kleva, Marco De Simone, Brian Dean, David Deane-Freeman, Andrew Del Biondo, Tony Del Busso, Lino Del Giudice, Peter Della Tolla, Selwyn Dembo, Cameron Demoy, Alf Dennemoser, Aiden Devlin, Rob Devlin, Gerald Dew, Ryan Dew, Serafino Di Giampaolo, Frank Di Giovanni, Tony Dib, Doug Dickson, John Dike, David Dillon, Frank Dipierro, Matt Ditchfield, Tom Dixon, Joel Dobson, Robert Doe, Mardi Doherty, Pat Donato, Scott Donnelly, Jerry Donovan, Mick Doolan, Bernie Doonan, Ben Dougall, Ian Dougall, Craig Douglas, Kate Douglas, Con Douros, Paul Dowling, Darren Down, Djerijk Drent, Mark Drew, Adam Dridan, Glenn Drought, Ian Dryden, Tom Duane, Lawrence Duca, Loredana Ducco, Catherine Duggan, Colin Dunn, Jim Dunn, John Dunstan, Richard Dyer, Catherine Dynan, Paul Eades, Michael Easton, Matthew Edgcumbe, Chris Edquist, Neil Edwards, David Elia, Elias Elia, Sam Elia, Tan Elia, Wayne Elliot, Greg Elliott, Arthur Ellis, Megan Ellis, Tony Ellwood, Ian Elso, Shane Esmore, Brian Esposito, Frank Estevez, Dallas Ewing, Megan Eyles, Leon Eyre, Tjip Faber, Robert Facchini, Fulvio Facci, Robert Facioni, Michael Fairlie, Gary Farrell, Jeremy Farrington, Peter Fearnside, Kevin Felmingham, Corey Fenech, Craig Ferguson, Jeanette Ferguson, Domenico Filazzola, Frank Filippone, Brian Findlayter, Alan Finney, Michele Finnigan, Emma Fisher, Judy Fisher, Scott Fitzgerald, Tom Fitzgerald, Jon Flanagen, Bill Fleuter, Daniel Flood, Philip Flynn, Maryke Foeden, Belinda Foreman, Les Foreman, Ray Forrest, Fortunato Forte, Carolyn Foster, Kabrina Foster, Gaynor Fox, Gerry Fox, Karen Fox, John Fragale, David Francis, Garry Franklin, Jennifer Fraser, Ben Fraser, Simon Fraser, Ken Frazer, Ross Freiberg, Con Frescos, Mal Fryer, Bruce Fuller, Ron Fuller, Jack Fullerton, David Fulton, Nick Gaal, Fabio Gagliardi, John Gal, Lorenzo Galati, Bernard Galbally, Chris Gallagher, Daniel Galtieri, Lena Gan, Barry Gange, Carrillo Gantner, John Garra, Mandy Garside, Wayne Garton, Chris Gauci, Godfrey Gauci, Ian Gavin, Matthew Gay, Grant Gaylor, Gavin Geddies, Tim Gellert, Erik Gelt, Chris George, Bernard Georgelin, Dhruvajyoti Ghose, Bob Giebels, Kirsten Gilbert, Lloyd Glanvill, Chris Glasgow, Alexie Glass, Catherine Gleeson, Shannon Gobell, Eleni Gogos, John Gollings, Kirstin Gollings, James Gonzales, Jerry Gonzales, Rod Gonzales, Debbie Goodin, David Goodman, Peter Goodman, Jack Gordon, Richard Goss, Peter Goudis, Costa Gouranos, Corey Gourley, Larry Govan, Anne Govic, Jaclyn Gow, Norm Grady, John Grasett, Dean Gray, Helen Greasby, Michael Grech, Greg Green, Corey Greenaway, Justin Greenaway, Kate Gregory, Ted Gregory, Olivia Griffith, Darren Griffiths, Matthew Griffiths, Jane Grimshaw, Mijke Groot, Philippe Grosjean, Stephen Grove, Joe Guario, Michael Guarnieri, Robert Gvildys, Elliot Gwyne, Kis Gyeui Janos, George Haddad, Trevor Haig, Dawn Hales, Tim Hales, Alex Hall, Brendan Hall, Cate Hall, Gary Hall, John Hall, Kathie Hall, Wendy Hamill, Geoff Hammonds, Natalie Hampson, Annette Handley, Luke Handley, George Hanna, Daniel Hanrahan, John Haralabakos, Nicole Hardman, Helen Hardwick, Dominic Harford, Michael Harnack, Lyn Harper, Michael Harper, Andrew Harpur, Trevor Harpur, Jihad Harrak, Andrew Harris, Garry Harris, Nick Harvey, Ros Harvey, Derek Hawkes, Shane Hawkes, Mark Haynes, Lyndon Hayward, Robyn Healy, Phil Heather, Jamey Hehir, Bruce Henderson, Mary Hennessey, Graham Herbert, Michelle Herrick, Martin Hicks, Jane Hider, Gerrard Higgins, Lyall Hill, Tim Hill, Anton Hillemacher, Khoo Hin, David Hingst, Anil Hira, Anita Hirschhorn, Damien Hiscock, Nhu Hoang, Troy Hoare, Warren Hoare, Paul Hobbs, David Hoctor, Tony Hodder, Prani Hodges, Marie-Laure Hoedemakers, Tyson Hofstee, Sean Hogan, Anthony Holland, Brett Holmberg, Peter Holmes, Matthew op't Hoog, David Hook, Robert Hook, Gregory Hope, Geoff Horan, Michael Horan, Tony Hore, Barrett Houston, Michael Howard, Rob Howden, Tom Hrelja, Olivia Hrvojevic, Andrew Hume, Ron Humme, Karl Hummer, Mark Humphries, Ben Hunt, Graeme Hunt, Lewis Hunt, Michelle Hunt, Ross Hunter, Timothy Hurburgh, Michael Hutchinson, Penny Hutchinson, Robert Hutchinson, Justin Hutchison, Leah Huynh, Bill Hyams, Angelo Iacopino, Sabri Ibrahim, Matt Icme, Serkan Icme, Irina Ilina, Hedley Imbert, Dylan Ingleton, Dr Alison Inglis, Sally Ingram, Con Ioannou, Adrian Irving, Mark Irving, Peter Jackel, Roy Jacob, Ron Jaegers, Stuart Jardine, Matt Jasionek, Steven Javens, Peter Jenkins, Steve Jennings, Bruce Johnson, Phil Johnston, Graham Jolly, Ben Jones, James Jones, Maureen Jones, Stuart Jones, Toni Jones, Stewart Joyce, Sarah Jury, Hans Kaehan, Stephen Kainey, Yiu Chen Kan, Con Karagiannakis, Kingsley Karunaratne, Adrian Keane, David Keegan, Mel Kelly, Merran Kelsall, Rosemary Kendall, Paul Kennedy, William Kennedy-Cooke, Brendan Kenny, Robert Kerr, Daniel Khong, Hin Khoo, Dean Kilpatrick, Adrian King, Judith King, Malcolm King, Andrea Kleist, Richard Klepac, Alan Knight, Colin Knowles, Lindsay Knowles, Simon Knowles, Ralph Koch, Roger Koch, Chris Korfiatis, Tina Koutrouzas, Peter Kowalyov, Ian Kozlowski, Robyn Krause-Hale, Michael Krivitsky, Nada Kula, Shan Kumar, Vera Kung, Olda Kurdiovsky, George Kustra, Leo Kuter, Reg Laan, Andrew Lacey, Daniel Lacey, Archie Laing, John Lake, Trevor Lam, Jerry Lamonica, Ashley Lane, Jason Lang, Libby Langlands,

Elizabeth Langley, Ann Lau, Frank Lau, David Lauder, Alex Lawlor, Jeff Lee, Angeletta Leggio, Les Lesko, Ian Lewis, Scott Lewis, Odette Li, Reno Lia, Stan Liacos, Ronny Liew, Fabian Lima, Frances Lindsay, Elke Link, Brad Little, Peter Lodding, Ian Logan, David Longo, Joe Longo, Simon Loone, Martin Looney, Adam Lord, Kevin Love, Roxane Ludbrook-Ingleton, Jon Luker, Norma Lund, Dizzy Lyle, Rachel Lynch, Jenny Lyndon, Stuart MacKellin, Antonio Madaffari, Peter Maddison, Scrooge Madigan, Hermann Mahler, Daniel Malacchini, Lyndon Malcolm, Rocky Malivindi, Glenn Malloch, Michael Malouf, Gus Mamar, Rosalea Monacella, Nicole Mandile, John Mangisi, Chris Manhal, Jim Manos, David Mapstone, John Marinaccio, Tony Marino, Stephen Marks, Maria Marques, Jodie Marshall, Reg Marshall, John Marta, Geoff Martin, Stuart Martin, Phillip Martin, John Martinez, James Martyn, Chris Maskiell, Brian Mason, Norm Mason, Svetlana Matovski, Nick Matveev, Esther Mavrokokki, Sharyn May, John Mayers, Carlo Mazzone, Robert Mazzone, Dugald McAndrew, Elsie McBean, Denise McCann, Brian McCarthy, Mick McCarthy, Richard McCarthy, Bill McCorkell, Jon McCormack, Bruce McCracken, Tim McCue, Adam McDonald, Holly McGowan-Jackson, Darren McGown, Kim McGrath, Rod McGrath, Stephanie McGurk, Graeme McInness, Jeff McIntosh, Len McIntosh, Ken McKay, Sian McKenna, Ian McKenzie, Adrian McKinnon, Ed McLaren, John McLean, Andrew McLerie, Peter McMahon, John McNabb, Duncan McPherson, Fiona McRobb, David McTaggart, Matthew McVeigh, Kylie Meacham, Bernie Meade, Tim Meakes, Anat Meiri, Tony Mele, Imants Melkis, Gerry Mendes, John Micaleff, Charlie Miceli, Patricia Michailides, Gaeton Mickalef, George Migios, Jessica Migotto, Dijana Mikovski, Michael Milburn, Kevin Mill, Jim Milledge, David Miller, Justin Miller, Russell Miller, Iain Milne, Ralph Milone, Cliff Minter, Dean Mitchel, John Mohan, Nicole Monteiro, Steve Montfort, Cassandra Montgomery, William Montgomery, Paul Mooney, Chris Moore, Cliff Moore, David Moore, Emma Moore, Gary Moore, John Moore, Matt Moore, Simon Moore, Raul Moreira, Andrew Morgan, Mick Morgan, Paul Morgan, Danny Morino, Andrea Morrissey, Gary Morse, Romy Moshinskhy, Celina Mott, Geoffrey Mould, Martin Mowlan, Merlin Muaremi, Peter Muaremi, Iven Muir, Scott Muir, Elizabeth Mulquiney, Barry Murphy, Leigh Murphy, Rick Murphy, Tim Murphy, Joy Murphy-Wandin, James Murray, Lauren Murray, Mandy Murray, Robin Murray, Rupert Myer, Paul Nagel, Paula Nason, Sue Nattrass, John Naughton, Matt Negrin, Jarrod Neilson, Lyndsay Neilson, Peter Nerone, Graeme Newcombe, Dominique Ng, David Nguyen, Trang Nguyen, Andrew Nicol, Con Nicolas, Vic Nicoli, Goran Nikolic, Scott Nolan, Chris Noonan, Rick Noonan, Tony Northover, Mark Notley, Tony Oates, Melissa Obeid, Andrew O'Brien, Leysa O'Brien, Paul Och, David O'Connell, Richard O'Connor, Grant O'Donnell, Johnathon O'Donnell, Mark O'Donnell, Lance Ogle, Johnny O'Hara, Gary Oliver, Tom O'Loughlin, Andrew Olynic, Vin O'Neill, Jim Opasinis, Tania Orr, Jason Orton, Genevieve Overell, David Owen, Dennis Owen, Mark Owen, Rob Pacconi, Julian Padgett, Helen Page, Tony Page, Luciano Palma, Craig Palmer, Maudie Palmer, The Hon John Pandazopoulos MP, Gina Panebianco, John Paniagua, Irene Papadimitrou, Peter Pardon, Jose Paredes, Tony Parisella, Fiona Parker, Chris Parkinson, Tom Parol, Mike Parry, Trevor Parry, Andrew Partos, Michael Paspalis, Vanessa Paspalis, Carolyn Patamisi, Stuart Paterson, Stuart Paton, Brent Patterson, Matthew Patterson, Tim Patterson, Shannon Pawsey, Stephen Payne, Claudio Paz, Walter Paz, Phil Pearson, Andrew Peavey, Alex Peck, Andrew Peck, Cristian Pedretti, Geoff Pegg, Sue Ellen Pepperall, Shannon Percy, Frederika Perey, Mardi Peters, Ross Petersen, John Peterson, Quoc Pham, Tri Phan, Terry Phelan, Anthony Philp, David Pickering, David Pidgeon, Rory Pincott, Andris Pinnis, Michael Pittock, Dennis Plainos, Ian Platt, Colin Pleydell, Matthew Plumbridge, Simon Pockley, Susan Pockley, Madhu Pokhrel, John Polatsidis, Chris Polendakis, Cobey Poletti, Andy Pollitt, Andrew Pollock, Hilary Pollock, Lyn Pollock, Toby Pond, Richard Ponsford, Roger Poole, Chris Poulos, Peter Powell, Adrian Pratt, Eric Preece, Mark Prentice, Carlene Price, Chris Price, Graeme Priest, Carl Priestly, Helen Privett, Elizabeth Proust, Theo Psomas, Shaun Purple, Mira Puspa, Chris Pyres, George Qing, Alan Quigley, Peter Rahilly, Janine Ralev, Francesco Ramigni, Ian Ransley, Annabel Rattigan, Bhaven Raval, David Rea, Shona Reaper, Simon Reed, Felicity Reeves, James Reid, Nathan Remyn, Kevin Renshaw, David Renwick, Vic Revell, Kate Rhodes, Michelle Rhodes, Tony Richetti, Ray Richards, Eric Richie, Clare Riddoch, Toby Rigiazz, Cr David Risstrom, Sav Rizzas, Pringle Robertson, Warwick Robertson, David Robinson, Damien Robinson, Troy Roda, Dick Roennfeldt, Jeremy Rogers, Jacqui Ronalds, John Ronaldson, Shane Rose, Steve Rose, Stuart Rossiter, Lachlan Rothnie, Bill Rouw, John Rowe, Chris Rowley, Cathy Royal, James Rubira, Fernando Rudas, Pradeep Rupanagudi, Joe Russo, Darren Ryan, Judith Ryan, Paul Ryan, Tony Ryan, Daniel Rybak, Andres Sanchez Jnr, Edgardo Sanchez Snr, Edward Sanderson, Pru Sanderson, Wayne Sanderson, Lisa Sassella, Juan Sastre, Evan Savio, Chris Sawyer, Jeff Sayers, Bianca Scaife, Gerlee Scanlan, Helen Schokman, Johnathan Scholes, Peter Schreuder, Kevin Schulz, Andrew Scott, Brian Scott, Michael Scott, Kelvin Seamer, Peter Seamer, Natasha Sebastian, Ian Seeley, Benjamin Self, Vince Selvi, Andras Selymesi, James Service, Mark Sewell, Michael Shanahan, Geoffrey Sharpe, Suzanna Shaw, Simon Sheedy, Matthew Sheehan, Mark Sheldon, Ann Sherry, Blair Sherwood, David Shultis, Kyle Sieble, Querubim Silva, Lawrence Simmonds, John Simmons, Andrew Simons, Daine Singer, Julie Singleton, Chris Siomos, Peter Skinner, Tom Sloan, Angelos Smagas, Russell Smart, Sally Smart, Mike Smillie, Cameron Smith, Chris Smith, Dale Smith, Damon Smith, Geoff Smith, Leigh Smith, Michael Smith, Noel Smith, John Smithies, Harry Sokol, Katie Somerville, Dave Spalding, Ron Spargo, Ivan Spehar, John Spellman, David Spencer, David Spiteri, Tim Stacey, Andrew Staedler, Nick Stakos, Zoran Stamenov, Marijana Stankovic, Marco Staub, Ian Steedman, Trevor Stephens, Keith Stevens, Peter Stevens, Andrew Stewart, Joy Stewart, Ken Stewart, Ken Stickland, Melina Stilo, Daryl Stonehouse, Anita Storti, Bill Stowenovski, Maria Stratford, Pat Strickland, Mark Strk, Rob Stuart-Smith, Colin Stuckey, Mike Subritzky, Chris Sundblom, Don Sweatman, Barry Sweeney, Barry Sweeney, Jeremy Sweet, Roger Sykes, Adrian Szentessy, Gabrielle Tabron, Damien Rammer, William Tannock, Philip Tantsis, Adrian Tarticchio, Warren Tassell, Deliah Taylor, Lei Tchin, Gino Tendelli, Mario Terlikar, Cuong Thai, Han Thai, Simon Thewlis, Bruce Thomas, Russell Thomas, Brad Thompson, Dale Thompson, Simon Thompson, Scott Thomson, Kate Thurgood, Simon Tiller, Graeme Tilley, Phil Tillyer, Tutura Timote, Ron Toal, Blythe Toll, Dean Tonkin, Phillip Torcasio, Bob Tracey, Quan Tran, Phu Tran Pham, Aaron Tranter, Ron Trapp, Harold Trappe, Antonio Travanca, Melinda Traves, Paul Treadwell, Georgie Tregear, Luis Trego, Andrew Trewern, Jules Tribuzio, Steven Tsikaris, David Turk, Ross Turner, Tim Turner, Stephen Tyack, Eric Utterback, Steve Utterback, Frank Van Dam, Jarrod Van De Laak, Rene van der Velde, Finn van der Velde, Hugh Van Essen, Adrian Van Gaal, Albert van Grieken, Susan Van Wyk, Mark Van Zuylan, John Vandenberghe, Anton Varga, Ron Varga, Gerard Vaughan, Tony Veal, David Vega, Simon Vella, Cosimo Vello, Pieter Verstraaten, Amber Victor-Gordon, Joe Vidak, Richard Viojo, Steve Vizard, Joe Volpetti, Glenn von Bibra, Paul Von Chrismar, Albert Voots, Oliver Voss, Ivan Vukelic, David Wagstaff, Paul Wagstaff, Peter Wakeham, Andrew Walker, Jeff Walker, Jenny Walker, John Walker, Karl Walker, Ronald Walker, Ross Walker, Vanessa Walker, Zione Walker-Nthenda, Ben Wall, Ben Walley, Ed Wallis, Kevin Wallis, Haydn Walsh, Peter Walsh, William Wan, Chris Wardle, Graeme Warland, Peter Washington, Robert Wastell, Barbara Watroba, Beth Watson, Chris Watson, Darryl Watson, Peter Watson, Lance Weatherell, Ross Weeks, Mark Weightman, Greg Weir, Jeromy Wells, Chris Welsh, Grant Welsh, Daryl West-Moore, Heidi Wharton, Danielle Whitfield, John Whitfield, Fiona Whitworth, Glenn Williams, Judy Williams, Paul Williams, Steven Williams, Thomas Williams, Adrian Wilson, Bill Wilson, Darren Wilson, Russell Wilson, Geoff Winnett, Stephan Wobking, Daniel Wollenburg, Nathan Wombell, Narelle Wood, Phil Wood, Trina Wood, Allan Woodall, Courtney Woodford, Joy Woodford, Brett Woodhouse, Jeremy Woods, Dave Worland, Dave Wright, William Wright, Sherrin Xerri, Mihalis Xidis, Peter Yates, Christopher Yerondais, Jenny Yim, Garry Yin, Gary Young, Ken Young, Robyn Young, Rohan Young, Mike Zafiropoulos, Nolan Zail, Jane Zantuck, Nancy Zhang, Jiong Zhu, Jim Ziarkas, Dirk Zimmerman, Paul Ziros, Rob Zukowski.

Part I: Selected Bibliography

Allan, J. Alex. 'The story of the Yarra', *Victorian Historical Magazine*, vol. 18, no. 72, Dec. 1940, pp. 91–112.

Anderson, Don, Dovey, Kim & Echberg, Bruce. 'Melbourne covers its tracks. Federation Square – Design competition winner', *Landscape Australia*, 4 (1997): 325–9.

Anonymous. *Melbourne as it is, and as it ought to be; with remarks on street architecture generally*, Reprinted from the first number of The Australasian, Revised, Melbourne: J.Pullar; Geelong: J. Harrison, 1850.

Bell, Agnes Paton. *Melbourne: John Batman's village*. Melbourne: Cassell Australia, 1965.

Bennetts, Don. *Melbourne's Yesterdays 1851–1901: a photographic record*. Medindie: Souvenir Press, 1976.

Borrie, E.F. *Melbourne Metropolitan Planning Scheme 1954*; Report. Melbourne, 1953.

Brown-May, Andrew. *Melbourne Street Life*. Melbourne: Australian Scholarly Publishing, 1998.

Critelli, Barbara. 'Federation Square: Melbourne's Civic Heart'. Honours Thesis, History Department, The University of Melbourne, 2000.

Dingle, Tony & Rasmussen, Carolyn. *Vital Connections: Melbourne and its Board of Works 1891-1991*. Ringwood: McPhee Gribble, 1991.

Evans, Doug. 'Federation Square; a long time coming'. *Transition* 57/58: 6–13.

Goad, Philip. *Melbourne Architecture*. Sydney: The Watermark Press, 1999.

Harrigan, Leo John. *Victorian railways to '62*. Melbourne: Victorian Railways Public Relations and Betterment Board, 1962.

Historical Records of Victoria, foundation series

Jones, Colin. *Ferries on the Yarra*. Melbourne: Greenhouse, 1981.

Lewis, Miles. *Melbourne: the city's history and development*. City of Melbourne, 1995.

Metropolitan Town Planning Commission. *Plan of general development Melbourne*. *Melbourne:* Government Printer, 1929.

Presland, Gary. *The Land of the Kulin*. Fitzroy: McPhee Gribble/Penguin, 1985.

Royal Victorian Institute of Architects. Journal of proceedings.

Victoria Centenary Celebrations Council Historical Sub-Committee. *Victoria: the first century: an historical survey*. Melbourne: Robertson & Mullens, 1934.

Weidenhofer, Margaret (ed.). *Garryowen's Melbourne*. Melbourne: Nelson, 1967.

Williams, Jenny. 'The search for a square' in Graeme Davison and Andrew May (eds), *Melbourne centre stage: the Corporation of Melbourne 1842–1992*, special issue of *Victorian Historical Journal*, 63, 2 & 3 (October 1992): 50–63.

Williams, W. Lloyd. *History trails in Melbourne*. Sydney: Angus and Robertson, 1957.